cost effective college

CREATIVE
WAYS TO
PAY FOR
COLLEGE
AND STAY
OUT OF
DEBT

cost effective college

GORDON WADSWORTH

MOODY PRESS

CHICAGO

To my wife, Janet,
for the many years of encouragement and sacrifice
she has bestowed on me and our three daughters,
Kim, Julane, and Tara

contents

foreword

A major concern for many college students today is the final accounting of their student loans when they graduate. What could be more crippling than to end up owing thousands of dollars the day you receive your degree?

While students and parents applaud the widespread availability of student loan programs, the reality is that this easy money plunges many students into oceans of debt. As more student loan money has become available, colleges have steadily increased their tuition fees. As Gordon Wadsworth points out in *Cost Effective College,* student borrowing could reach $52 billion per year by 2002.

The outpouring of student loans has already begun to take its toll. The loan default rate is the highest in history and some turn to loan consolidators to work out a schedule of payments that could last up to thirty years.

Many times I hear of young people who want to serve the Lord in ministry but are financially enslaved because of debt. When the misuse of credit becomes an overwhelming burden, nearly everything else goes out of balance as well. Using our money wisely, even during the college years, is commended by Jesus: "He who is faithful in a very little thing is faithful also in much; and he who is unrighteous in a very little thing is unrighteous also in much" (Luke 16:10).

Students can earn a degree today without going into debt. *Cost Effective College* offers numerous suggestions on grants, scholarships, and alternative funding for all students whether they plan to attend a small Christian college, an exclusive private school, or a large state university. I encourage every student to read this book before filling out a college application.

ANDY STANLEY
Pastor, North Point Community Church
Atlanta, Georgia

acknowledgments

Iremember well one night in 1973 when a friend brought a newcomer to our home Bible study in Atlanta. The guest had just moved to our city with his family, having joined Campus Crusade for Christ. His message was different. He spoke about money and how it all belonged to God and that we are to be good stewards. This was a new concept for me, something I had never heard before. But I am firmly convinced that the Lord sent Larry Burkett to us that night and I continue to be blessed by his message to this day. His concepts, carried forward today by the organization he founded in 1976, Christian Financial Concepts, underlie the key premise of this book: Students and their parents can and should strive to be debt-free in every enterprise they undertake, including the financing of a college education.

A special thanks to everyone at Christian Financial Concepts, especially Larry Burkett, Joe Coney, and Chuck Thompson. Were it not for these men and others in the ministry, this publication would not be possible.

A special thanks also goes to those who have given so much of their time, encouragement, and financial support over the years, including Roger Adams, Sam Conway, Ross Greene, Mel Guinn, Rick Hasty, Jeff Hall, and my brother, Jim Wadsworth. I have been greatly blessed by these men and continue to learn more from each of them every year.

I also want to thank Jim Vincent at Moody Press for putting up with me during our many hours of fine-tune editing of this manuscript, and to Jim Bell, acquisition's chief at Moody for his encouragement and support in bringing this concept to fruition.

And finally, to my wife, Janet, for her dedication and commitment in perusing and editing each original chapter over the past two years.

introduction

THE CLIMBING COST OF A COLLEGE EDUCATION

I magine one group of adults borrowing $50 billion dollars a year for four years, most of them unable to work full-time on a regular basis, and all of them receiving in exchange a wealth of knowledge and thinking skills but no tangible products. Is that a fair trade?

Millions of college students and their parents think so, and the long-term dividends are substantial. But the immediate costs are great—and getting greater. Predictions are that in 2003 it will cost $16,500 to attend a state college or university for one year, or more than $66,000 to earn a four-year college degree. By 2010, a four-year education at a state school will be upwards of $90,000; for a private school, the price tag will be an astounding $180,000.[1] (To see projected near-term costs, see appendix 1.) And while parents want to help the students with the major costs of college, the burden of paying has been lifted from the parents and placed squarely on the shoulders of the students.

Meanwhile, many families, already weighted down with multiple car payments, a significant house payment, credit card debt, and rising taxes, probably welcome the reversal of responsibility. But the news is not good. The large loan limits—up to $65,000 for undergraduate students and an additional $73,000 for graduate students—and the relative ease in qualifying—mean many students can and are graduating with major, long-term debt. And parents suffer watching (and trying to help) their college graduate struggle with finances as he or she begins a career.

Taking out student loans should be the last resort, as we will discuss in chapter 11. Regrettably, if analysts are correct, student borrowing will rise to $52 billion annually by 2002, forcing thousands of students into financial bondage.

To graduate from college without debt will require discipline as well as strategic planning. Next to buying a home, paying for college can be the greatest financial challenge students and their parents will face. Unlike a home, which can be amortized over three decades, college tuition payments must be paid prior to every quarter or semester.

Although many factors are involved in selecting a school, finances often dictate the final outcome. Financing your child's (or your) college education is a valid concern, and this book will show you how to do it without accumulating an enormous debt.

A BRIEF HISTORY OF SPIRALING EDUCATION COSTS

If you're a parent who attended college years ago, you may wonder how costs climbed so high so quickly. Certainly the cost factor was far less of a concern before the mid-1980s. Prior to that time, consumers were able to keep more of their spendable income, surrendering less to the government for taxes, social security, and Medicare. In addition, the state schools were heavily subsidized and could offer a well-rounded education for a minimum investment. Equally significant, the federal government had not yet entered the student loan business, which today only helps to proliferate tuition costs.

The question most parents pose today is simply, "Why?" Why did tuition suddenly soar in the 1990s, and why does it continue to increase on an annual basis? One of the reasons is directly related to the lack of state subsidies. With funds once set aside for higher education now being used for the construction of new prisons and paying for rising state Medicaid costs, many schools have been forced to increase tuition fees to fund the deficit. Some states have now legalized gambling and offer a state lottery in the guise that the money is primarily for education; some funds go there, but not enough to end the march in tuition increases.

Security, fuel, and labor costs also continue to rise on most campuses. Many of the older buildings on American college campuses are in need of renovation or replacement. At the same time, the demand for new research and computer labs is at an all-time high. In addition, Uncle Sam opened the floodgates to more government-backed student loans in 1992 with the unsubsidized Stafford Loan that allows significant borrowing without regard to family income. This not only tempted students to borrow money beyond their means to readily repay, but, as a source of student funding, the Federal Stafford Loan furthered tuition increases, much to the detriment of the average student. Add to this the government's continued promotion of the Stafford Loan as an entitlement, and you have the formula for hyperinflationary costs and growing student debt.

SOME BASIC STRATEGIES

Pursuing a college diploma represents one of the most demanding four or five years of a person's life. Most students, in hindsight, would say it was well worth the investment of time, money, and emotion. What, then, can students do in order to graduate from college without a millstone of debt around their necks?

Strategic planning and discipline are key components to avoiding debt upon graduation. That planning may necessitate attending a community college prior to transferring to a four-year institution. Many students opt for one or two years at the local college before transferring to the four-year school. Others follow the two-year school with service in the military. The loan payback programs in the military are excellent and remind me of the athlete who receives a signing bonus. To be able to go to college while being paid seems like a responsible solution for students with limited resources.

Another strategy that is becoming more acceptable among students is selecting a college or university that best fits their aptitude as well as the family budget. Many are finding it beneficial to consider schools based on their relative academic prowess with other incoming students; this can increase their likelihood of qualifying for certain grants or scholarships at a particular institution. In other words, if a student appears only average at one college but far above average at another, the second college is more apt to offer early acceptance as well as some form of institutional financial assistance.

These and many other strategies will be discussed in this book to eliminate or greatly reduce financial indebtedness upon college graduation. One philosophy behind selecting a school reflects an opinion held by many parents: Enroll at a school because of its reputation.

Occasionally, students apply to highly esteemed schools simply because of the school's reputation and the recognition afforded them. Perhaps their reputation as a business school is unsurpassed; they're ranked in the top five in library science; or several well-known state and national leaders have graduated from their prelaw course. *That sure would look good on my résumé,* the student thinks.

While I do not concur with that philosophy, there can be no doubt that some schools bring to mind a sense of superiority. Years ago my brother earned his master's degree in finance from a state college in California and was then hired by Merrill Lynch in New York. Shortly after starting his new career, he felt uncomfortable telling coworkers where he had earned his degree. "When I told them, they just looked at me in amazement," he said. "They expected me to say Wharton, Yale, or Harvard."

While big-name schools look impressive on a student's résumé, rarely do employers base their hiring decision on a student's alma mater. Like America's top schools, employers also seek applicants with noteworthy character qualities, work experience, and leadership. College grades are important, but not nearly as important as a well-rounded applicant who demonstrates a great deal of promise.

A PREVIEW OF THINGS TO COME

During the 1980s and 1990s, as our three daughters moved through high school and into college, my wife and I came face-to-face with the task of finding student financial aid for our daughters. We quickly discovered that much of the information available was bogus. I immediately encountered all the phony claims of unused scholarships and college funds that were supposed to save us thousands of dollars. Finally, I became so annoyed and infuriated with the entire process that I started my own financial aid service.

As I began doing extensive research concerning student financial aid, I prepared a simple guidebook for people who wanted to know what to do and whom to trust. A year later I introduced a two-hour seminar in public and private high schools and was occasionally asked by banks to speak to their collective audiences. Later I took the guidebook to Larry Burkett at Christian Financial Concepts in Gainesville, Georgia. That meeting not only changed the way I perceive student funding but also greatly altered the work that is now part of *Cost Effective College*.

This book will help parents plan for their children's education, and it will help students avoid financial bondage. Included are real-life stories of students and parents who took bold steps to avoid or escape financial entrapment. (All names have been changed.)

Chapters 1 and 2 will offer strategies for choosing and applying to the right colleges. "Choosing a College" includes the exciting story of a student who "packaged" his qualifications for acceptance into one of America's finest universities. "How To Apply for Financial Aid" lets both students and parents look into the world of student financial aid at both secular and Christian colleges. The chapter also explores the reason why some students receive scholarships and grants while others are only entitled to student loans.

The sought-after Pell Grant and Federal Supplemental Educational Opportunity Grant are both featured in chapter 3, "Student Grants and Work-Study Programs." In addition, an illustrative story describes why the federal work-study program is a "win-win" for everyone involved. And in chapters 4 and 5 you will learn about general and specific scholarships. "Scholarship Programs," chapter 4, unveils where to apply and how to get the attention of those who read every application and judge the winners. Included are specifics relating to the federal government's Hope Scholarship, two specific national scholarship programs, and important tips on writing essays while applying for the thousands of dollars available from America's finest entrepreneurs. "Athletic Scholarships," chapter 5, offers strategies for student-athletes to qualify and remain legally eligible with the collegiate athletic associations plus several resources and addresses, including on-line recruiters, for learning about schools and financial aid to athletes.

Planning ahead for a career in education, nursing, social work, or law enforcement allows students to borrow up to $40,000 at no cost when serving in a specialty area for five years, detailed in chapter 6, "Service-Cancelable Loans: Loans that Become Grants."

Chapter 7, "Alternative Funding," explores the benefits of cooperative education. For the co-op student who combines work and study, the savings can be thousands of dollars. In addition, we'll look at Uncle Sam's own version of cooperative study; for those students who meet the strict qualifications for certain federal positions, the U.S. government offers to pay all tuition fees plus a sizable monthly stipend and a guarantee of employment upon graduation.

Chapter 8, "Military Options," looks at another option: winning scholarships from the military in return for future service, and opportunities to serve as a military reservist on weekends while earning a comfortable monthly wage. The chapter also presents a student loan program that enables a student to pay back up to $65,000 in student loans in only three years.

Chapter 9, "Money Management for Students," contains practical helps for students and recent graduates to avoid debt, including an income/spending plan, steps to balancing a checkbook, and tips on how to avoid the "credit card trap." Meanwhile, parents can learn about saving for their child's college education in chapter 10, "Strategies for Paying for College." Savings programs include certificates of deposit, educational and Roth IRAs, and custodial accounts; and we will see how compounding can cause such savings to grow over the long-term when left untouched.

In "The Last Resort," chapter 11, we go behind the scenes to reveal the "real cost" of the low-interest government loans and why they should be avoided whenever possible. We'll learn, for example, that the average student who chooses to remain in college and earn a graduate-level degree is permitted to borrow up to $138,000 from the federal government without any credit qualifications or assets. And while the government is very lenient when it comes to handing out taxpayer money for student loans, it offers no leniency when it comes to student loan repayment. Much like an income tax debt owed to the Internal Revenue Service, a student loan cannot be canceled through a bankruptcy. Therefore, it is critical that students are aware of their overall responsibility and regard such loans as a last (and limited) resort.

Finally, for those unable to attend on-campus college classes, "About Distance

Education" explores the world of virtual campuses—campuses without walls but featuring computer-assisted learning that really teaches. This is a legitimate way for students to earn their bachelor's or master's degree from an accredited school while avoiding a massive debt load.

Please note that the information provided has been checked for authenticity and accuracy prior to publication. Nevertheless, all programs, grants, scholarships, on-line addresses and application forms noted remain subject to change. (For instance, over time, some scholarship amounts may actually increase!) All figures are accurate for the years noted. Furthermore, the mention of specific programs, colleges, or universities does not imply an endorsement by the author or the publisher.

EXPLORING THE OPTIONS

The ways to fund an education surely have changed through the years. When I was in college, there were no search firms or financial aid packages; you simply made it on your own. In my senior year, my schedule permitted me to work thirty-five hours per week for a large international advertising agency in San Francisco. During that year, I received my best grades while acquiring experience that would stay with me for the rest of my life.

Today the options are different, though there are similarities. Our three daughters had college work-study jobs, and they would not hesitate to admit their experiences were very rewarding. In fact, they had to compete for their campus positions, which included a key place in the student union, conducting campus tours for visiting high school students, and working as a lifeguard at the university's new aquatics center.

With all three daughters at a university just a short distance away, we were able to enjoy many college activities with them. Being part of the campus life was more than just great football games, women's soccer tournaments, inspiring concerts, parents' weekends, and cookouts. It was also a success story of trusting God for fifteen academic years of college, free of financial bondage.

You too can find success in funding your children's (or your own) college education. Join me as we look at the above topics, as well as consider appendices with sample applications and valuable tables, charts, and forms. Throughout the book you will find dozens of on-line addresses for scholarships and other kinds of financial assistance, and tips that can save you thousands of dollars.

Of course, the journey to higher education begins by choosing the right school. For that, let's turn to chapter 1.

NOTE

1. Adapted from "Planning for College," a brochure from Met Life Resources of Metropolitan Life Insurance Co., 1996. Annual increases have been adjusted based on a 5 percent rate of inflation.

chapter one

CHOOSING
A COLLEGE

Your son is a junior in high school and looking forward to an exciting and fun senior year. He may not be thinking about college. But he should be, and so should you. Once he does, he will learn this truth: One of the most challenging aspects of a high school student's life is finding a college that best suits his needs, desires, and ambitions.

How hard is it? Some students spend years visiting colleges across the nation. Others move quickly toward selecting their parents' alma mater or a school attended by a brother or sister.

Ryan Kelly, a promising young student-athlete from California, took the first approach. When he was only a freshman in high school, Ryan started looking at college catalogs and literature. Then beginning in his sophomore year, Ryan and his father, Richard, began visiting various colleges that had provided key information regarding admission requirements.

Richard Kelly was a successful entrepreneur and had invested money for Ryan's college education for several years. His wife, Lynn, also contributed to their college savings plan, and together they were able to save a substantial amount of money in hopes that they would not have to accept student loans from the government. (For more information on college savings and prepaid tuition plans, see chapter 10.)

As a student, Ryan was just outside the top 10 percent of his high school class by the end of his junior year. As an athlete, he had been a quarterback on the freshman football team and a varsity player on the school's volleyball team. Together with his tough schedule of classes, Ryan spent many hours practicing with his team each day, which helped him to develop discipline and time-management skills.

In addition, Ryan spent over nine years in scouting, receiving the organization's highest honor as an Eagle Scout. In his final year of scouting, he was elected the senior patrol leader, presiding over one hundred scouts and eventually earning a recognition award for outstanding leadership. This character development would later prove beneficial in his quest for college admission, as would the ten advanced placement and honors classes Ryan mastered during his four years of high school.

A TWO-YEAR OR FOUR-YEAR SCHOOL?

Ryan's parents recognized the benefits of a college education; they knew a two- or four-year college degree would be essential in today's climate in order to achieve economic success. Their son would soon face the same decision most high school students confront as they consider the right school: Should they go to college for two years or four—or more? In fact, many companies today require their new employees to hold at least a master's degree, with some emphasis also placed on having a doctoral degree (or being in a doctoral program). Guided by a student's interests and aptitude, a high school guidance counselor can assist in directing the student to the college that will best fit his or her career objective. See appendix 2 for a sample listing of careers available for students with an associate's, bachelor's, or master's degree.

Likewise, those not interested in earning a bachelor's degree or even an associate's degree can still benefit by pursuing advanced technical study at a junior college or trade school. In addition to taking the basic core courses in high school, those students may enroll in multiple occupational and technical courses such as welding, cabinetmaking, auto repair, or metal shop. With the help of their high school guidance counselors, the students can develop a college profile that combines the students' interests and economics, enabling them to recognize their own aptitudes and interests, choose the appropriate college major or the appropriate technical career path, and save thousands of dollars in government loans. This can set the stage for both a future vocation and little, if any, student debt upon graduation.

Flexibility can be the key in the college selection process. Many families do not have savings available for college like the Kellys; these parents and students often resort to borrowing almost 100 percent of the funds from the government. Instead, they could turn to a combination of two- and four-year schools. Thus, students willing to attend a local community college for their first two years prior to transferring to the big-name school can save significant sums.

Rhonda Morgan, associate professor of business administration at Gordon College (Barnesville, Georgia), asked students to consider the cost and educational benefits of attending a two-year school first:

> What if you could save almost half the cost of a college education? Suppose you choose to begin your college education at a two-year community college? A student could complete the first two years of a four-year degree at a fraction of the cost of a four-year school. Then, after two years, the student could transfer to a four-year college or university.
>
> Studies comparing the achievement of two-year college students with four year colleges and universities have found that the more courses students take at the community college level, the better they do in a four-year school. . . .
>
> After two years of study at the community college, the Bachelor's degree can then be pursued at a four-year college or university. In the end, the Bachelor's degree comes from the "school of choice" without the high tuition costs for all four years.[1]

THE RIGHT HIGH SCHOOL COURSES

Key College Requirements

Part of preparing to choose a college is choosing appropriate classes during high school. Many colleges and universities today look for a minimum of sixteen to eighteen units of college preparatory classes. The basic courses that most colleges require are: English, four years, including English composition, American, English and world literature; math, three to four years, including geometry, algebra I and II, and trigonometry (calculus is recommended); history and geography, two to three years, including U.S. and world history, U.S. government, world cultures, and civics; and lab sciences for two to three years, such as biology, earth science, chemistry, or physics. Colleges also expect some fluency in a foreign language, acquired by studying at least three years of French, Japanese, Russian, Spanish, German, or Latin, for example. In addition, students should choose such electives as economics, computer science, art, music, communications, psychology, and drama.

Some of the above courses, especially in the sciences and mathematics, are offered as honors and advanced placement classes, providing high school students a sneak preview of college-level work in many different subjects. The classes cover extensive material at a faster pace, presenting a stimulating challenge for motivated students.

Advanced Placement Classes

Students who complete advanced placement classes help their college future in several ways. First, they improve their overall application profile. Most colleges view advanced placement courses as a sign of the student's willingness to accept a challenge and proof of their intellectual competence. Second, students who score a grade of three or higher (out of five) in an advanced placement examination, given at the end of the course, may receive college credit from the prospective school, which can save hundreds or even thousands of dollars in tuition fees. (More selective schools require a grade of four or higher.) Even if the student does not score high on the exam (or chooses not to take the optional exam), he or she can enhance the grade point average by earning a grade point higher than the traditional four-point scale. In other words, a student who earns an A in an advanced placement class scores a five-point grade; a B is posted as a four-point.

A Focus on Academics

By the time Ryan Kelly completed his freshman year of high school, it was apparent that his interests and abilities were especially keen in mathematics. Because of his stringent schedule, there was very little time for cruising the mall or watching television. He was bright, but not brilliant. Yet he excelled in every math class available and continually scored high in the math section of the Scholastic Assessment Test.

The Kellys continually encouraged their son and sacrificed in many ways in order to provide for strong academically-based primary and secondary schools. They were always amazed at his teachable attitude and carefully nurtured his self-motivation.

"Your grades need to be among the highest, and you need to limit your television watching to weekends if you want to get into a good college," said Lynn Kelly, Ryan's mother, an education administrator.

Like the Kellys, many parents start planning for college when their student is still in middle school. If you're a parent, you can begin planting college seeds when your child is twelve or thirteen. If you're a student, begin with your freshman enrollment and choose classes that will help you get ready for college. Remember that the best schools demand a full schedule of college-prep classes. It makes sense to plan years in advance for the type of courses to be taken in high school.

QUESTIONS TO ASK ABOUT THE PROSPECTIVE COLLEGE

Beyond the academic preparations, students need to focus their college choices by asking the right questions. Determining where to spend four or five years on one campus prompts questions like, "Will I fit in?" and "Will I be challenged?" Students visiting a college in person should ask pointed questions of the administration, as well as query the students to learn what life is truly like on their particular campus.

College-bound students should divide their questions into the following five categories, listing the "pros" and "cons" for each college: (1) the distinctive nature of the school, (2) the academic reputation, (3) geographical location, (4) the student body, and (5) the overall size of the campus. First, though, they should ask the primary question: "What type of school do I want to attend? Do I prefer a two-year community college, a four-year liberal arts school, a Christian college, or a technical institution? Do I want a nationally recognized state university, a small private college, or a famed Ivy League school?" Ultimately, students should choose a college where they fit both spiritually and academically.

Then the student can begin asking the questions in each category. For instance, under the academic reputation, the student could ask, "Does the school offer a major that interests me? Does the campus provide an environment for learning? Is the school ranked scholastically? Will I be challenged academically, and more importantly, will my faith be challenged? What are the average SAT and ACT scores of incoming students? Do my national test scores meet or exceed the scores of others? Is there an up-to-date resource library and research facility? Are there academic, professional, and/or Christian organizations on campus?"

Other questions for determining academic standards are: "What is the ratio of students versus faculty? What percentage of all classes do professors teach versus graduate assistants? How many professors hold a Ph.D.? Are the classes small and intimate or taught in large lecture rooms? What is the average number of students per class? Do the professors have an open-door policy for assisting their students? How easy is it to change majors and does the school provide professional counselors for every student? What is the retention rate? What is the current graduation rate?"

Thinking ahead to graduation, some students may ask, "Is there a graduate school attached to the college or university? If so, what percentage of graduates apply for graduate school? Do the academic standards match my aspirations and allow me to achieve my designated goal after graduation? What does the school do to help graduates find jobs? Do they have a reputation for advancing graduates into key positions with Fortune 500 companies?"

Among the questions concerning the student life are these: "Does the school provide adequate dormitories or will I be required to live in off-campus housing? What kind of meal plan is offered in the dorms? Is the dormitory coed? If so, how is the gender separation handled within the dorms and bathrooms? What kind of health facility is available? Does the college or university provide up-to-date computer labs? Do most students have desktop computers or carry laptops to class?"

The geographical location is often a deciding factor for many students who prefer to be near their home rather than days away by car (or several hours away by costly jet travel). If the school is out of state, a student is likely to ask, "Is the cost of transportation figured into my overall budget? Is the school located in an urban or rural setting? Is the community slow paced or is it primarily academically focused? Finally, how safe is the campus? What are the crime statistics for the campus and surrounding area?"

Some students prefer a large school, while others want to know everyone on campus and enjoy a feeling of camaraderie. More questions might be: "How large is the student body? What is the ratio of male to female students? Do most students return home on weekends? Is the campus a walking campus, a bicycle campus, or do I need an automobile? Are automobile expenses figured into my overall budget? Are there sororities and fraternities on campus? If so, what percentage of the student population are members and would I need to become a member to fit in? What do the students do for fun? What percentage of the student body is involved in intramural and varsity sports? During my visit, were the students helpful and congenial or arrogant and unfriendly?"

Of course, don't overlook questions regarding costs and probability of acceptance: "What are my chances for acceptance? Will admittance to the college be a stretch or am I assured of enrollment?

"Can I apply for state residency after the first year and begin paying in-state tuition rates? Is the school affordable based on my budget? Is it possible to receive an institutional scholarship award? What percentage of all students qualify for financial aid? Can I qualify for work-study? Will my AP credits transfer?"

With so many questions to be answered, students should seek counsel from their parents, teachers, guidance counselor, coaches, and local youth pastor. The Bible is a crucial resource for the Christian student. I especially recommend Proverbs 2, particularly verses one through seven, as the student weighs his choices.

VISITING THE CAMPUS IN PERSON—OR BY COMPUTER

Richard Kelly and his son were determined to visit as many college campuses as possible to learn the answers to scores of their questions. In fact, between Ryan's sophomore and senior years in high school, Ryan and his father toured nine colleges and universities.

"Our two campus trips around the country were possibly the best one-on-one times I ever spent with Ryan," the senior Kelly later told a friend. "Driving between colleges allowed ample time for debriefing, analysis, and reflection. It was also a great opportunity to discuss Ryan's spiritual values and the potential impact of the various environments on those values."

Unlike the Kellys, many students do not have the time or money to visit several colleges across the country. For those students, the Internet is a welcomed friend. At www.campustours.com, students can take a virtual tour of hundreds of colleges without ever leaving their home and without ever spending money for plane tickets, hotels, and rental cars. And many schools have their own web sites, usually under www.*schoolname*.edu that includes information on the student body, location, information on courses (often from the catalog) and photos or a video tour of the campus. (The school name may be abbreviated on the web site; look at application information.) If you don't have a computer, usually one is as close as a local library or your school's computer lab.

PREPARING FOR THE SAT AND ACT

Referring to the attention given the national testing program, G. Gary Ripple, director of admissions at Lafayette College in Easton, Pennsylvania, noted, "There is such a great variation among high schools in the quality of teaching, the quality of courses offered, the quality of textbooks and the consistency of grading policies, that admission committees perceive SAT/ACT scores as a common denominator. While standardized test scores are not as important as the high school transcript, they serve as a convenient screening device for admission committees faced with thousands of applications."[2]

Because of the increased competition for institutional scholarships and admission into the best colleges and universities, students should consider receiving tutorial assistance prior to their final national test date, regardless of whether they attended a Christian school, private academy, a public high school, or were schooled at home.

At the beginning of his junior year, Ryan prepared to retake the SAT exam. It was a personal challenge, and the Kellys had provided a tutor, confident the private help would be able to give Ryan's verbal score a boost. All were disappointed when the boost amounted to only 40 points, but rejoiced knowing that he scored a perfect 800 on the math. Ryan next tackled the SAT II and again scored high on the math portion but a dismal 570 on writing.

Other assistance can help students get ready for the big assessment exams. Of particular note is the Princeton Review, which offers courses in major cities to help students become more competitive in maximizing their PSAT, SAT, SAT II, or ACT scores. For those who are not near one of the Princeton Review testing centers, the agency also publishes dozens of college prep books, including *Cracking the SAT, 2000 edition; Cracking the SAT II: Spanish;* and *Cracking the SAT II: Physics.* In addition, they publish the average test scores for incoming students at hundreds of colleges and universities across the country. Interested students may contact them on the Internet at www.review.com or by calling 800-2REVIEW. Internet-active students can also check out the Kaplan Educational Center for books on testing preparation at www1.kaplan.com.

COMMUNITY AND EXTRACURRICULAR SERVICE

Before their first trip to visit several college campuses, Ryan's father wondered, *With so much emphasis placed on class ranking, could the college possibly determine that Ryan is just outside the top 10 percent?* Ryan had a strong 4.2 (out of 5.0) grade point average, but his dad feared that class ranking would be viewed as a negative. *Even though his perfect math score looks good, his final SAT was still shy of 1400. Will they knock Ryan out because of his poor showing in verbal and writing?*

Fortunately for Ryan and thousands of other high school students, grade point averages and scores on college entrance exams are not the only factors receiving weight. Extra activities are very important. In fact, several of the schools visited by the Kellys expounded on the need for extracurricular activities. "One thing we learned on our first trip across the country was the significance placed on community service," commented Richard.

Involvement in school and community activities is so important to colleges that many have designated scholarships for students directly involved. For example, Rhodes College (Memphis, Tennessee) provides a four-year scholarship for students who have demonstrated a high level of commitment to community service. Winners of the Bonner Scholars Program make a commitment of ten hours per week to service projects and service-learning activities and select summer service projects, jobs, or internships around the world. The award includes a stipend of $3,500 per year.

Rhodes also offers the Lucius E. Burch Leadership Scholarship designed specifically to reward students for their commitment to leadership in community service. Those selected participate in a four-year leadership development program and commit to at least ten hours of public service weekly and involvement in the leadership development program. Each of the ten recipients receives a $10,000 scholarship per year in addition to any other Rhodes grants and scholarships.

"Although Ryan was active with his church youth group and had taken part in work projects in Mexico, only a couple of the schools we visited seemed to relate that to community service," Richard later recalled. "What did matter was the mental note we took of the groups that the universities deemed valid. There were two organizations we felt particularly comfortable with; namely, Habitat for Humanity and Special Olympics."

At that point, Ryan and his dad made a pact. If Ryan was going to participate in the community projects, then dad would too. Over the next year, the two Kellys assisted Habitat for Humanity in building a new home for a low-income family and remodeling another that was once a former drug house. Additionally, they worked with the track-and-field group of the Special Olympics' organization.

"Both were real eye-openers," said Richard. "Each of us came away with increased awareness and appreciation for those who live in crime-infested neighborhoods and especially those with mental and physical disabilities. It was truly a blessing for us both."

During the summer between his junior and senior years in high school, Ryan had another eye-opening experience, visiting a leper colony in the Dominican Republic while serving on a work project. "I've never seen anything like that before. I was very moved," Ryan solemnly reflected. "But the really neat thing was their attitude. They never complained and were very grateful when we visited them."

Students are frequently encouraged to pursue extracurricular activities such as after-school sports and even part-time jobs, proving to the admissions staff that they are well-rounded and capable of improving the college community. Multiple activities also indicate a proficiency in managing different roles.

The Kellys were somewhat surprised to hear one admissions director express a different opinion concerning incoming students, "You may have heard that we are looking for well-rounded students. On the contrary, we are looking for students who have excelled in a specific area, possibly a sport or a talent. Combining these 'specialists' with other classmates provides us a well-rounded student body."

Most of the schools the Kellys visited had a similar challenge: "If you have any aspiration for attending this university, you need to register for your school's most demanding courses and show us outstanding results."

"We also learned that in addition to the course curriculum, the colleges take a close look at the overall competition in each high school as well as the scholastic reputation and their history with the college," Richard acknowledged.

"Eventually, I came to the conclusion that every student should have a complete dossier in order to attract the attention of the admissions committee, who wade through thousands of applications," Richard added. "I then realized the importance of Ryan packaging his accomplishments and abilities to make himself more appealing to every admissions committee."

HOW TO PREPARE IF YOU'RE A
HOME-SCHOOL STUDENT (OR TEACHER)

This same concept can be especially helpful for students schooled at home and seeking college acceptance. According to Cafi Cohen, author of *And What About College?*, home-school families may even have an advantage in the application process "Just as home-school parents have customized their educational philosophy and their student's interests and goals, families can tailor their application to focus on the student's strengths,"[3] writes Cohen.

While colleges and universities use the same criteria in evaluating students, such as grade point average, admissions interview, essays, SAT and ACT test scores, awards, and recommendations, those schooled at home may have an edge over students with a transcript filled only with academics. "A student with only a paper trail of academics risks being lost in the crowd and does not necessarily come out on top when competing for slots at selective colleges," adds Cohen.

Cohen believes that home-schooling parents should give equal weight to a student's activities and academics. When addressing home-school audiences, she reminds parents "not to restrict themselves to government high school requirements and to look for ways to exceed those requirements in areas where the student is talented and gifted.

"Admission officers are becoming increasingly interested in those who are home schooled, and the alternative programs help demonstrate to the admissions committee that the student far exceeds common high school standards," says Cohen. "With good documentation, a home-schooled student with average academic backgrounds and standardized test scores will have little trouble gaining admission."[4]

According to *The Campus Life Guide to Christian Colleges and Universities*, Christian colleges are more likely to agree with the philosophical reasons for home-schooling, and many are actively recruiting home-schooled students.[5]

As noted by the Kellys on their tour of higher education institutions, colleges want a wide diversity of students on their campuses, and students who have been educated at home certainly add to that diversity.

Regarding transcripts and applications for America's best colleges and universities, Cohen states that the more selective schools need written proof or documentation of home-schooling, i.e., portfolios, transcripts, standardized test scores, letter of recommendation, interview reports, and student essays. "Two types of family-generated documentation commonly accompany college applications from home-schooled student: a portfolio or a transcript," notes the author.

Because some states still struggle in their acceptance, home-school parents need to be prime record keepers, documenting every scholastic achievement and accomplishment. "Some colleges and universities consider themselves highly innovative and often seek students with non-traditional backgrounds and documentation. For these schools a portfolio submission usually impresses admissions officers," writes Cohen.[6]

In many cases, portfolio submissions do appear risky and may present time problems for the admissions office that may already be bogged down with thousands of applicants. Based on her experience, Cohen suggests a custom-built transcript that highlights a student's work as well as his or her activities and projects. In her book, Cohen provides parents a complete how-to guide including establishing high school credit hours, sample transcripts with exhaustive course descriptions, application essays, cover letters, detailed résumés, and more.

THE APPLICATION PROCESS: WHEN AND WHERE

Every year, beginning in September, colleges and universities across the country begin reviewing applications submitted for the following fall semester. In some cases, up to 30 percent of the applications are submitted under "early decision" rules. If accepted, early decision candidates are required to firmly commit to attending the school and immediately withdraw all other college applications.

While most schools won't admit it, early decision applicants often have an advantage, especially if the student would otherwise be marginal based on his or her credentials. The reason is primarily economic; the college or university can know by mid-December how many students are securely committed and how many openings still remain.

The application procedure is similar in almost every school. Whether the application packet is submitted in the fall for early decision or in the spring with the remaining application pool, the submitted papers are quickly scrutinized to see that every required component is included. If not, the application is returned to the student for additional processing. In most cases, the applications are read as soon as they arrive (another reason for students to submit their admissions request early).

If the application is complete, most schools appoint two or three members of the admissions committee to review the contents and score the applicant based on the student's performance. For example, a student could score a seven or eight on academics, a six or seven on teacher and counselor recommendations, but only a three on extracurricular activities. Every aspect of the application is scored prior to going to the full committee for acceptance or rejection.

While not every student is afforded an interview with the admissions official, any personal contact with a college representative can prove beneficial. When the Kellys heard of an informational meeting in their city sponsored by one of the schools Ryan and his father had visited, they planned to attend, hoping for a personal introduction to the campus representative. Their time was well spent. Later they learned that the same representative also sat on the university's admissions committee.

Some schools send recruiters to various parts of the country to make contact with students at their high school or at one of the many college fairs. College fairs offer students the opportunity to visit with representatives from numerous schools at one specific location. Those who attend are able to ask key questions of each representative and collect brochures, applications, and even detailed information regarding scholarships and student financial aid.

One recommended strategy is to apply to more than three schools. In fact, most high school guidance counselors recommend that students apply to as many as five different colleges, since more than 70 percent of all students file admission applications in the spring of their senior year. For example, two schools may be more selective in their admissions criteria and possibly a stretch or marginal for acceptance. Two others may be considered "80 percent chance" schools, while the last college is labeled a "safety school," one where the applicant knows in advance that he or she will be accepted.

PREPARING THE ENTIRE PACKAGE

As Ryan rounded the corner for his fourth and final year of high school, he made a decision where he would like to attend college. Even though he knew he might have a difficult time qualifying for admittance, Ryan chose a private northeastern university as his number one choice for early decision. He also selected another nationally recognized university as a second choice, and since that school had a non-binding early action option, Ryan elected to apply to both schools concurrently.

Facing the SAT II a second time, the Kellys offered Ryan additional testing assistance and a great deal of prayer. The results: a boost of 130 in the writing segment and a whopping 750 on the math IIC. Now he felt ready, and his excitement was almost contagious.

The Kellys realized that *everything* was important to the admissions committee, including community service time, grades, essay, recommendations, and even a thank-you note to each of the schools they had visited. To be sure Ryan's package was complete, they prepared a checklist, complete with the necessary dates for each item to be submitted. (For a sample checklist, see appendix 3.)

Wise students will request letters of recommendation as early as possible. Provide your references with the name of the admissions director, the school name and address, and the deadline for each letter to be submitted. Most letters of recommendation come from high school guidance counselors or teachers who have taught you and are familiar with your talents, abilities, attitude, and performance. Other meaningful letters may come from coaches, employers, a principal or headmaster, or even the student's pastor, all of whom are able to communicate the student's character qualities, growth potential, and drive toward success.

Over the next few weeks, Ryan labored extensively, struggling with the two applications, especially the essays. Both schools required a very formal application and two distinct essays, one dealing with the student's decision to attend the school, and the other more open-ended. Ryan chose to write about his days in the Dominican Republic and his experience with Habitat for Humanity. He provided drafts to his English teacher, as well as friends and family, to review. Ryan eventually rejected those segments that were starting to sound like a reading of *Roget's Thesaurus*.

Not every college requires a student to submit an application essay, but those that do place a considerable amount of importance on the writing.

As the deadline for the two applications grew closer, Ryan began to feel the pressure and stress. He had not applied to a "safety school" where acceptance was highly likely, thinking he'd have good chances by applying for an early decision with one school and early action with another. "If they both turn me down . . . well, I guess I'll just have to go back and look at some of the other colleges," Ryan humbly told some of his close friends.

WAITING TO HEAR . . .

While Ryan waited to hear, his father continued checking off each component on the checklist they created to be sure nothing was overlooked. "We have to be sure your credentials are stellar and we have covered all the bases," Richard told Ryan. "Let's see . . . the transcripts have been sent, your test scores are in, your letters of recommendation are mailed. Now we just need you to wrap up your essay and we'll be ready to go."

One night in early December of that year, they received a late-night phone call from the West Coast representative for one of the universities. He had called to verify Ryan's new SAT II scores and inquire how Ryan was doing in his senior year with three AP classes. He also revealed that Ryan's application would be presented to the entire admissions committee the following day.

Nearly everyone in Ryan's circle of friends told him the same thing, "Watch for the 'thick' envelope," they said. "It's the one that has all the housing forms and other campus information. That will be your acceptance package."

When Ryan stopped at the mailbox several days later, he was taken aback when he found only a small, thin envelope from his second-choice school. Slowly and hesitantly he opened the envelope, and much to his delight and surprise, he had received their welcome and acceptance.

The following day he again received a thin envelope, this time from his first-choice school. He knew it could not possibly contain any housing or other information. He felt very disappointed and did not open the envelope. Somewhat emotionally, he continued to stare at the outside of the envelope as he walked unhurriedly into the house. *Could it be that they too only send thin envelopes like the one I received yesterday?* he speculated.

Finally, knowing that at least he was accepted at one school, Ryan slowly and almost methodically opened the envelope, and then suddenly let out a shout. "Yes!" He had been accepted to his first-choice school, a highly recognized Ivy League university. Moments later, the entire Kelly family paused in prayer to give thanks.

"When Ryan first made the decision to apply to two large universities, he knew he would have to give up his hopes of receiving a volleyball scholarship," commented Richard. "We were really proud of him. He felt he could play at a smaller college but decided on those two schools strictly because of the academics."

In the weeks that followed the ordeal, Ryan and his parents often reflected on the overall process and results. "What made the difference?" they inquired of each other. *Some of his grades could have been higher, and certainly a higher SAT would have helped,* they thought.

"The difference?" Richard responded. "The difference was twofold; first, God's direction and guidance and, second, Ryan successfully presented himself as a complete package!"

NOTES

1. Rhonda Morgan, "Two Plus Two," *Money Matters*, January 1997; published by Christian Financial Concepts, Gainesville, Georgia.
2. G. Gary Ripple, *Do-It Write,* 5th ed. (Alexandria, Va.: Octameron Associates, 1999), 6.
3. Cafi Cohen, *And What About College?* (Cambridge, Mass.: Holt, 1998), 29. Also available by writing the author at 160 Cornerstone Lane, Arroyo Grande, California 93420, and enclosing $19.95 (includes shipping) payable to *And What About College?*
4. Ibid., 24–25.
5. Mark Moring, *The Campus Life Guide to Christian Colleges and Universities* (Nashville: Broadman & Holman, 1998), 153.
6. Cohen, *And What About College?* 56.

chapter two

HOW TO APPLY FOR FINANCIAL AID

Carol and Bill Forsyth rarely contemplated the subject of finances. They had both grown up in the Midwest, and neither of their mothers worked outside the home nor made money of a topic of conversation. Years later, their family backgrounds and personal experiences in college would make them unprepared for the issues in funding their own children's college education.

Both of Carol's parents were born on a farm and grew up very conservative politically and very prudent financially. Even though money was never discussed in front of Carol or her brother, it was Carol's belief that when the time came to pay for college, her parents would have the money to take care of everything.

College cost much less then. Carol's parents' long-term savings plan meant Carol had all her expenses paid when college began, plus a small allowance every month for spending money. Although she did not have a car on campus, she was pleased to be able to go to the private university of her choice.

Bill's story was different. He attended a state university, where tuition was more reasonable, even minimal, thanks to the vast state funding of colleges and universities at the time. Years later, it would be hard for him to realize how much tuition had climbed in the more than twenty years since he had graduated. He also had developed a lifestyle during college that would be difficult to maintain years later.

Bill had joined a fraternity upon his arrival at college. Soon his college funds ran short and he had to get a job in order to maintain his lifestyle. It was a humbling experience when he starting working in the fraternity house kitchen in order to pay for his room and board. Soon Bill's mother became very sick, and most of the money that had been set aside for Bill's education was now being used to cover high medical costs.

To help supplement his earnings as a dishwasher at the fraternity house, Bill got a job working at a local men's store which helped to provide for his updated wardrobe. That seemed important; several of his fraternity brothers often talked about their "new threads," a term they used to describe their trendy wardrobe.

Bill's mother lost her battle with cancer. Even as he grieved, Bill knew he had lost the rest of his parents' financial support. After only three years of college, he volunteered for military service in the army.

Years later, Carol and Bill met in California and eventually married. Both had graduated from college by that time, Carol debt free, Bill with student loans. Nevertheless, Carol's budgeting techniques helped to successfully free them from past debts and eventually provide for a home.

Bill was very assertive in his sales position, but also aggressive in his spending habits. Even though his income was somewhat limited, Bill never learned to plan ahead, and his insatiable desire to have new things often seemed out of control. Eventually there was a larger automobile and a bigger house to accomodate an expanding family. Once when his sales exceeded his quota, he received a sizable bonus; he insisted that they buy a condominium in Florida, which he referred to as an investment.

"We'll make a bundle on this," he told Carol enthusiastically. "This location is hot and when we're not using it, we'll just rent it out."

Carol was not thrilled about the idea. "I hope you're right," Carol told him somewhat reluctantly. "I think we're taking too big a risk. That's all the money we have." Carol wished they had never taken that vacation in Florida that led to such a risky investment. "He is so impulsive," she often said.

Soon the Forsyths' debt began to escalate, and Carol's dream to have money saved for their three children's education faded into the distance. Whenever the conversation would come up about the condominium, Bill would often go into a tirade, blaming everyone but himself concerning their financial problems. "If the economy hadn't taken a downturn, it would have been a lot different," said Bill. "Besides, how did I know my job would be cut and we'd have to sell our house and condo at a big loss?"

When their children were toddlers, it didn't seem to make much of an impression on Bill to hear about tuition costs going up. Now, however, their oldest daughter, Stephanie, had begun to talk about college, and the pressure was starting to build.

"We're hoping to find some scholarships for Steffie," Carol told her friends at a PTA meeting somewhat nervously. "Even though Robby is only in the ninth grade, he is already talking about going to college too."

Carol didn't want to admit to anyone at the meeting that they had absolutely no money saved for Stephanie's college. What she didn't know was that most of the parents at the meeting had the same problem. "I'm not sure what we're going to do," she said. "Have you heard about all those scholarships that never get used?" Several women said they had heard the same story, but no one knew where to find information or how to apply.

FINANCIAL AID FORMS: THE FAFSA AND CSS PROFILE

Financial aid for college, whether scholarship, grant, work-study, service-cancelable loan, or some other financial assistance, is highly diverse, composed of a mosaic of public, private, and institutional sources. Some of the types may be better suited for a student than others, as we will see. However, no matter what type of aid the student applies for, the process is the same: a highly structured procedure, one that needs to be carefully adhered to. If errors are made or the proper forms are not filed on time, there can be extended delays and even the loss of grant money.

The first thing to determine is which financial aid application is required by the college. Some private schools, for example, will not consider any government aid, refusing all forms of federal grants and student loans. The schools that hold to this philosophy maintain their independence from Washington and eliminate the restrictions such programs can place on a school—restrictions that have limited other educational institutions. These schools make their beliefs well known; they have deep convictions that Uncle Sam should be a distant relative when it comes to any kind of handout. They want "no strings attached" when it comes to Uncle Sam's programs. As a result, they provide their own financial aid form for incoming students.

Whatever the aid you seek—whether from the school directly or outside agencies—you will probably need to complete a Free Application for Federal Student Aid (FAFSA). Most colleges and universities want all incoming students, whether home-schooled or schooled in a private or public school, to file the FAFSA after January 1 of the desired award year. The preprinted FAFSA is available from college financial aid offices and high school guidance counselors, and accounts for some ten million financial aid forms processed annually. See sample in appendix 4.

Both students and parents are required to indicate their adjusted gross income, assets, federal taxes paid, the number of members in the family, the number attending college at least part-time and the age of the older parent. Some people feel that the information requested by the government is an invasion of their privacy. Because of this, those parents refuse to apply for any federal assistance. And, of course, those schools that do not participate in government aid programs typically will not require the FAFSA.

A student whose parents are divorced or separated needs only to indicate the income of the parent with whom he or she resides most of the time. If that parent remarries, the stepparent's income must also be shown, even if the stepparent provides no financial assistance or support.

The student should mail the completed form to the central processing center indicated by the college. Four to six weeks later, the student will receive a copy of the student aid report, revealing the family's expected financial involvement prior to any assistance. The report also indicates the student's eligibility for the Federal Pell Grant and the Federal Supplemental Educational Opportunity Grant.

An even faster way to submit the requested information is to log on to www. fafsa.ed.gov and complete the "FAFSA on the Web." Only one application is necessary regardless of the number of colleges receiving the information. Each student submitting an application on-line will receive his or her own PIN to help speed up the process. The U.S. Department of Education hopes to substantially increase the use of the Internet for students seeking financial aid in lieu of the millions of paper forms submitted every year.

After the colleges receive the student aid report from the central processing center, the financial aid staff analyzes the information to determine what type of financial aid package to offer each student. A student's financial need, as defined by the government and colleges, may be met by a combination of grants, scholarships, loans and/or a work-study program. When the schools put together financial aid packages, they are unique for each student.

Many private schools want information not requested on the federal application form, including the value of the family residence. Therefore, in addition to the federal form, those institutions require students to complete the financial aid profile from the College Scholarship Service, the financial arm of the College Board. The cost of the Profile is $7.00 for registering plus $16.00 for each school that receives the information. A sample appears in appendix 4, together with the FAFSA.

For a highly desirable student, a school may use the "expected family contribution" figure generated by the federal form. For another student, the school may use the second financial aid form, the CSS Profile, which would increase the family's contribution by adding home assets to the formula, thus reducing the amount of institutional aid available.

The Forsyths' debt problem did not develop overnight but was definitely exacerbated when Bill invested all their savings in the condo in Florida. Eventually, the Forsyths made an appointment with a financial counselor. Bill introduced their three children and then admitted that they had been unable to save any money.

"It seems like every dollar we get goes right out the window," said Bill. "We've tried to save, but it just hasn't worked out. You know, in one pocket and out the other," he nervously joked. "Now we also have to consider what to do about Robby in a few years."

"Robby is really doing great in school right now," Carol added. "He's getting super grades and, of course, Steffie too." Both Robby and Stephanie nodded their heads in agreement. Carol continued, "Is it true there are a lot of scholarships that no one ever claims?"

The counselor quickly dismissed that report as a story some scholarship search firms have used in their sales pitches in order to lure unsuspecting parents into spending hundreds of dollars in their quest for student aid.

"I wish that were true, Carol," the counselor said. "I get asked that so often. Unfortunately, it's just a myth that's been spread around for many years. The truth is, there is very little scholarship money that goes unused. If there is money left over, it's primarily exclusory corporate money that is not available to the general public. That doesn't mean, however, that scholarships are unavailable. It simply means you have to know where to look and how to apply," he added.

While the family listened intently, Megan, the Forsyths' bubbly seven-year-old, was playing just outside the window. She was running and kicking her soccer ball, totally disinterested in the information she would need for college entrance in a few years (including, perhaps, a soccer scholarship).

SAVINGS STRATEGIES: PRECOLLEGE ASSESSMENTS AND FINANCIAL MANAGEMENT

The Forsyth family is not unusual. Very few families today have enough money saved for college. Studies indicate that only 25 percent of all college students graduate in four years. A major reason for the low graduation rate is that students often change majors as many as three times while in college. This increases the number of years needed to graduate, of course, but it may also add between 20 and 33 percent to the total cost of the student's education.

With the low four-year graduation rate, many students are encouraged to accept the federal Stafford Loan as a means to pay for the increased financial burden. Any federal loan creates debt upon graduation—the higher the loan amount, the greater the debt. As we will note in chapter 11, this is a bad policy, a strategy that should be adopted only as "a last resort."

A Precollege Assessment

One way to avoid this dilemma is through a comprehensive precollege assessment. One program that can help in this assessment is called "Career Direct" from

Life Pathways, a career counseling organization in Gainesville, Georgia. Students are asked to answer questions relating to interests, skills, values, and personality. Once finished, the four-part assessment is returned to Life Pathways for a complete twenty- to twenty-five-page personalized analysis. This can help the prospective student determine his greatest interest and narrow his decision on a college major, helping him to find the right major the first time.

Life Pathway also offers a *Guide to College Majors & Career Choices,* which may be purchased separately or included with the assessment report. The book offers details on various college majors from accounting to zoology.[1]

Financial Management

Parents can also help their students save money for college by adopting prudent financial management in using their credit cards. Both Bill and Carol frequently used their credit cards to supplement their income. This created unnecessary debt that undermined their efforts to save for Stephanie, Robby, and Megan's education.

Here is where a financial counselor can help develop a spending and savings plan. The counselor helped the Forsyths establish a plan that included paying off their financial obligations and eliminating any unplanned spending. Part of the plan included meeting with a reputable nonprofit organization called Consumer Credit Counseling Service.[2]

On behalf of the Forsyths, Consumer Credit Counseling Service contacted the banks and worked out a repayment plan for each of their credit cards. Much to Carol and Bill's delight, two of the three credit card companies dropped all late charges, all over-the-limit charges, and even lowered the finance charge to zero percent. The third bank agreed to drop their interest rate to 10 percent, which was far better than the 19 percent the Forsyths were paying.

To help pay off their debt, Carol started a new job working in an upscale florist shop. However, when her salary was added to Bill's income, the expected-family-contribution level increased. Carol was surprised to learn that in working to help pay the credit card bills, she and Bill now were expected to pay a larger amount of Steffie's college bills.

HOW THE GOVERNMENT DETERMINES A STUDENT'S NEED

Defining Financial Need

Unfortunately, the needs analysis methodology used by the government does not always reflect a family's ability to pay nor their debt load and overall need. Neither family medical bills nor secondary tuition fees are taken into consideration when calculating the expected contribution. How the "need'" is met, of course, is a decisive factor in determining whether a student will graduate without debt. But determining the level of that need is crucial.

The government's definition of "need" is the difference between the "expected family contribution" (EFC) determined by an analysis of the student's FAFSA data and the actual cost of attendance. As an example, if the expected contribution is $4,500 and the student plans to attend a local college, financial need may not be indicated. The reason: A local community college may only cost around $2,000 a year. If the expected family contribution is set at $4,500, it suggests that the family has the money and will be able to pay the entire cost.

If, however, that same student plans to attend a school where the tuition, room, board, and books cost approximately $17,000, the difference of $12,500 is then determined to be the student's financial need ($17,000 less the $4,500 expected family contribution).

Certain students are considered "independent" and are required to include only their income on the federal application form. This generally lowers the EFC and increases the opportunity for a Pell Grant. There are very specific rules governing independent status. Unless students meet the qualifications for independent status (shown in appendix 5), they are considered dependent, even if they no longer live with their parents nor receive financial support. Self-supporting students who do not qualify as independent are encouraged to appeal directly to the financial aid administrator at the college.

About the EFC

Keep in mind the principle at work: All student financial aid is directly related to the EFC, except merit-based scholarships. In the case of merit scholarships, a student with a superior national test score plus an outstanding grade point average may be offered institutional aid from the college primarily in the form of scholarships, while another student may find his or her financial aid package replete with government loans.

To give the academic appeal a boost, many guidance counselors believe that students should apply to schools where their national test scores, scholastic achievements, and grade point average put them well above the freshman average.

Because the EFC is based on both income and assets, there is a cutoff whereby some students may have an EFC too high to qualify for a Pell Grant, usually somewhere in the $3,400 range (based on the year 2001). See samples of EFC estimates and the address for a free on-line analysis in appendix 5.

Students and parents are often surprised at how much the student's income and assets affect the expected family contribution. This was especially true for the

Forsyth family. Some years before Stephanie started planning for college, Carol's mother began sending each of the grandchildren a large cash gift every birthday. The Forsyths invested the money, and eventually each child had approximately $9,000 in savings. When shown on Stephanie's contribution estimate, over a third of her savings, or $3,150, was added to the EFC figure.

Ideally, grandparents desiring to assist in college finances should either give the money to the parents to use for the student's needs or wait until graduation and help pay off the student loans. Money given directly to the grandchild or put in a trust fund for the student will be considered part of the student's personal assets and will count against the student when applying.

Likewise, parents are encouraged not to borrow from their retirement account since those assets are shielded from the needs analysis formula, as are tax-deferred annuities and whole-life policies.

The rule governing assets within the family is twofold. First of all, the government expects 35 percent of all assets held in the student's name to be used each year for tuition and other college expenses. On the other hand, assets held in a parent's name are figured at only 12 percent, effectively lowering the family's contribution and opening the window for additional financial aid. In addition, parents should also avoid any capital gains or bonus income during the years their students are in college. Both increase the EFC and may reduce the amount of financial assistance.

Families with extensive cash assets that could increase the family's contribution may want to consider reducing their assets by paying off any credit card debt, automobile loans, or even a home mortgage. Additionally, it is wise to utilize the student's assets first before filling out the FAFSA. For example, students could use their savings to pay for an automobile, dorm refrigerator, microwave, compact disc player, computer, or even new computer software needed for future college classes, none of which will be considered in the needs analysis formula.

THAT "AWARD LETTER"

During the spring and summer months, colleges send students a notification of financial aid, often called the "award letter." This letter reveals the kind of aid being offered the student for the following academic year. For recruiting purposes, some schools may provide a preliminary financial aid package in the fall of the student's senior year in high school, pending verification of the student aid report.

Should the amount and type of financial aid shown in the award letter be unsatisfactory, a student may appeal the decision of the college by meeting with the head of the financial aid department where he or she has been accepted. Not everyone receives special considerations, but enough do to warrant the time and effort.

Over the years, the college financial aid administrators have been given more authority and responsibility for handling the thousands of dollars that pass through the financial aid office. With proper documentation, the aid administrator may adjust the components that determine the expected family contribution at his or her discretion. Individual special circumstances must exist and be documented before the school's aid administrator can make a professional judgment. Whatever the outcome, the final decision is left to the administrator and may not be appealed to the U.S. Department of Education.

AID PACKAGES AT CHRISTIAN COLLEGES

What financial programs are available at Christian colleges? That's the question Stephanie began to ask beginning in her junior year.

Applying to a Christian college is no different from applying to any of the hundreds of secular institutions across the country. For those seeking student financial aid, the procedure is also the same. Applicants are required to file the FAFSA, the CSS Profile, or the school's own financial aid form as described earlier. Many of the schools are listed in the book *The Campus Life Guide to Christian Colleges and Universities*. Since each college has a web site, students can start their search on-line.

Among the advantages of a Christian college education are overseas study programs. Christian colleges lead the nation in offering students the opportunity to study beyond America's borders. In fact, more than half of the schools affiliated with the Coalition for Christian Colleges and Universities provide students with an international study term and Christian outreach around the world. Reportedly, 85 percent of the students at Goshen College in Indiana spend thirteen weeks in a foreign country learning the language and customs while living with a host family and doing service work. Such study programs represent regular course work with no payment for the students' service; however, students enrolled continue to receive financial aid like any other student.

Work-Study and Work-Credit Programs

Many of the Christian schools today offer a variety of financial aid programs, just as the larger public colleges and universities do. For example, numerous students at Toccoa Falls College in northeast Georgia are reducing the cost of their education by assisting local school districts with literacy needs through the America Reads program. Through this special Federal Work-Study program, students can earn up to $2,500 per year tutoring kindergarten through third grade students in reading and math.

For those ineligible for the Federal Work-Study, Toccoa Falls offers a work-credit program where most of the income earned may be placed directly into the student's account for tuition, books, or related expenses.

Pensacola (Florida) Christian College, which has declined federal student aid, citing concerns over government requirements for eligibility, offers a variety of financial aid arrangements, including a strong work-assistance program. The school reports that about 50 percent of the nearly 4,000 students are paying for their own college education through its work-assistance program. Students can earn up to $2,800 per year to help offset the school's very affordable $5,000 annual sticker price.[3]

Use of Grants, Loans, and Institutional Scholarships

Many schools have creative and diverse aid programs. Here are just three. (Remember, specific amounts and percentages are subject to change.) Westmont College, located on 130 wooded acres overlooking Santa Barbara, California, offers an interest-free loan to California high school graduates with financial need based on the information gathered by the FAFSA. In addition to the Pell Grant, the service-cancelable Perkins Loan, and the Federal Work-Study program, Westmont College also offers incoming students institutional grants and scholarships based solely on academic achievement. At present, 60 percent of all students receive student financial aid that is not repayable.

At Taylor University in Upland, Indiana, students may be eligible for such federal financial aid programs as federal grants and the Federal Work-Study program that can provide up to $1,800 per year. The Church Matching Grant and the Christian Leadership Scholarship reflect the school's desire to assist those who show a great deal of academic and spiritual promise. Students may receive a Church Matching Grant of up to $750 per year for any funds contributed from a church or parachurch organization. In addition, those who demonstrate exceptional leadership skills and experience, and document this on their application and through their references, may be eligible for a leadership award worth up to 25 percent of tuition annually.

Incoming students in the top 10 percent of their high school class with an ACT score of 29 or a combined SAT score of 1300 may be eligible for the Taylor University President's Scholarship worth 15 to 25 percent of tuition, renewable annually. Those who score slightly less on the national tests and rank in the top 15 percent may qualify for the Dean's Scholarship worth from 10 to 15 percent of tuition.

Wheaton College, located in suburban Chicago, offers four-year ROTC scholarships as well as merit scholarships based on SAT/ACT scores. In addition to federal grants and multiple work-study programs, Wheaton has an assortment of private donor scholarships, including the President's Achievement Award for freshmen finalists in the National Hispanic Scholar Program and the National Achievement Scholarship for Outstanding Negro Students.

To help parents and students with tuition and fees, Wheaton has an installment plan available for monthly and/or deferred payments. Illinois residents may qualify for a state scholarship worth up to $4,500. There is also a special grant for students planning to become missionary doctors or nurses.[4]

AN ANSWER FOR STEPHANIE

Whether she enrolled in a public, private, or Christian school, Stephanie understood the funding challenge. Stephanie's high school allowed her to leave every afternoon and work at one of the local merchants. (The only stipulation for the work release was a quarterly report from the merchant to the school concerning Stephanie's performance.) However, the government mandated that half of a student's earnings over $2,200 be added to the EFC.

Her parent's EFC already was high, limiting her eligibility for certain financial aid. Her mother was shocked by the EFC estimate. "We have so much need," Carol said. "Surely there must be a mistake." There was not, but there was a solution. Fortunately for the Forsyths, Stephanie was only a sophomore in high school when they began to work on lowering the family's contribution. For one thing, Carol reduced the number of hours she worked at the florist shop and volunteered to help every week at her church office.

With Bill holding to an established budget, the Forsyths' debts soon began to disappear. Bill then took a wise, proactive position. He moved Stephanie's assets into Carol's and his name, including those given by Carol's mother. They now were required to pay federal taxes on the earnings generated each year; but this change allowed the Forsyths to determine how and when the money should be disbursed, rather than permitting the government to decide. That decision, along with Carol decreasing her salaried hours, soon caused the expected-family-contribution estimate to drop from $7,600 to less than $3,200. They also learned that once Robby started college, Stephanie's contribution would be cut nearly in half. This is based on the rule that substantially reduces the expected family contribution when two or more family members (excluding parents) attend college at the same time, even at different schools.

During the fall of Stephanie's senior year, Carol and Bill began to visit colleges with Stephanie. One by one they toured the campuses, first on-line, then in person. Before each campus visit, Bill phoned the school and made an appointment with the head of the financial aid department. While Stephanie enjoyed seeing each of the schools and talking with people on the admissions committee, in the end, it was the students at one particular Christian college that really motivated her to apply to that school.

Based on her class rank, SAT scores, and grade point average, Stephanie felt confident that she would be accepted at her first-choice school. Nevertheless, as a backup, Stephanie also applied to a college closer to her home that had been recruiting her over a period of some fourteen months.

Ultimately, both colleges sent her a letter of acceptance along with a notification for an institutional scholarship from the financial aid department. However, it was their daughter's first-choice school that especially impressed the Forsyths because an admissions committee staff member took the time to telephone Stephanie in person to tell her of the school's acceptance. And with a low EFC and the collegiate scholarship, the financial puzzle had fallen nicely into place.

NOTES

1. For more information on "Career Direct" or the *Guide to College Majors* book, write Life Pathways, P.O. Box 1476, Gainesville, Georgia 30503 or call 800-722-1976.
2. For information and the nearest location of the Consumer Credit Counseling Service, call 800-388-2227.
3. For additional information, contact Toccoa Falls College at 800-868-3257 or visit its web site at www.toccoafalls.edu. Further information about Pensacola Christian College and its work-assistance program can be obtained at 800-PCC-INFO or its web site, www.pcc.edu.
4. To receive further information on admission and student financial aid, contact Westmont College at 800-777-9011 or on-line at www.westmont.edu; contact Taylor University at 765-998-5206 or on-line at www.tayloru.edu; contact Wheaton College at 630-752-5005 or on-line at www.wheaton.edu.

chapter three

STUDENT GRANTS AND WORK–STUDY PROGRAMS

Married during the prosperous Reagan years of the 1980s, Paula and Jack Hansen wanted all the things their parents had. Unlike their parents who once put quarters into Laundromat machines and lived in one-bedroom apartments when they were first married, Paula and Jack demanded a better lifestyle from the very beginning.

"Why not?" Jack once told his friends. "We both have good jobs and our income is way more than my mom and dad ever had."

With their lofty combined income, the Hansens were able to qualify for a large home in one of the better neighborhoods in their community. As a matter of course, it also seemed quite natural to join the city's finest country club.

Both Paula and Jack worked for several months looking for the right kind of connection that would enable their application to be considered by the club's stringent membership committee. It wasn't until Paula became friends with the vice president's wife that she found someone who would give them a sterling recommendation.

"It costs so much to join, but just think of all the 'right' people we'll meet," Paula said to Jack. "You just have to make those connections." It was this same attitude that would ultimately lead the Hansens into financial difficulties.

Jack felt out of place each time he drove into the club's parking lot. While his car seemed very acceptable in his neighborhood, it just didn't fit in at the club. *I'll bet a lot of these cars are leased,* Jack told himself. *I can do the same thing. Besides, it won't take much to convince Paula. She loves the German imports.*

Months later the Hansens visited with Jack's parents, where Jack Sr. discreetly asked his son about their lifestyle. At first he was hesitant. He didn't want to seem combative, but he was very concerned. He knew what it was like to mismanage finances and hoped his son would not have to experience what he had gone through some twenty years before.

"Dad, it's OK," Jack said matter-of-factly. "Things are really coming together for us right now. I just received a raise and Paula may get moved upstairs anytime. But that's not all," Jack added, his voice rising with excitement. "I have this deal going on a boat you won't believe. You and Mom are going to love it. It's perfect for entertaining clients and I can even write it off."

Mr. Hansen's grim face revealed his displeasure. He glanced at his wife and could see that she shared his emotions. They were certainly not interested in any kind of boat that might lead their son and his family into financial bondage.

The move upstairs for Paula was not exactly what she had planned on. In fact, when the Hansen's first child was born and Paula was unable to return to work as soon as she had hoped, the top position was given to someone else. Paula was devastated. "I worked so hard for that! That should have been my spot," she exclaimed.

Over the years, Paula and Jack's family grew to four. Unfortunately, they had not planned well for all the added costs, nor had Jack planned ahead for the time when Paula would leave the workplace to be at home with their two children.

As financial pressures started to build and credit card bills continued to mount, the Hansens soon found their marriage in trouble. Each one admittedly blamed the other for their problems, and both found friends who would rally to their side for support. Carol blamed Jack for not keeping the checkbook balanced; she also thought he didn't need to have "expensive lunches every day." Jack said Carol had to stop playing golf with "your lady friends all the time."

Their fifty-two inch television with "that multispeaker surround-sound thing," as Carol called it, was just one of several signs of their trying to keep up with the latest creature comforts. Unfortunately, the home entertainment center had greatly extended the balance on two different credit cards.

Such comforts probably would need to be sacrificed as the Hansens considered upcoming college costs. With two growing daughters, Jack and Paula had considered having a budget and saving for the children's education, but Jack never made it a priority to develop a budget.

A REALITY CHECK

The Hansen's oldest daughter, Emily, began to think about going to college when she was a high school sophomore. Mom and Dad completed a financial aid form the following year, requesting an estimate of what the colleges expected them to contribute for Emily's education. The estimate revealed that, even though they were inundated with debt, their income was too high for the Federal Pell Grant. The Pell is basically an entitlement grant based on a student's established need, U.S. citizenship, and enrollment in an undergraduate course of study. Since the grant is directly linked to the expected family contribution, it does not take into consideration personal debt payments, high medical expenses, or private school tuition payments.

Jack and Paula were stunned. With all their credit card debt and Paula's so-so income, couldn't the people who calculated the estimated family contribution understand the contribution couldn't be that high? *Oh, well,* Jack thought, *it doesn't matter. Something has to give.* Eventually Jack heeded someone's advice that they see a financial counselor.

THE PELL AND THE SUPPLEMENTAL EDUCATIONAL OPPORTUNITY GRANTS

The Pell Grant wasn't an immediate option for the Hansens, but it is a good program for many with a moderate expected-family-contribution calculation. As one of the government's biggest programs, the Pell is available to all undergraduate students or students taking postbaccalaureate courses required for teacher certification. Some families with income well above average, who would normally have a family contribution of $3,000 or more, may qualify for the Pell because of the number of members in their family, the number of family members in college, or because of the amount they pay in state and federal taxes. Keep in mind that some students who are turned down one year may qualify for a Pell Grant the following year.

If a student selects a school that allows federal assistance, every family should file the Free Application for Student Aid—commonly known by its abbreviation as the FAFSA—regardless of income and assets. The FAFSA will generate an estimate of the expected family contribution, a figure used by administrators of the Pell and other grants and scholarships.

Should family income be reduced because of unusual circumstances, i.e., job loss, divorce, or major illness, the student may qualify for a Federal Supplemental Educational Opportunity Grant in addition to the Pell. Like the Pell Grant, the FSEOG is campus based, which means that Uncle Sam provides the money directly to the colleges and universities, who then distribute the funds to those with the greatest need, up to $4,000 per year. The Pell and the FSEOG are grants, not loans, meaning the funds are gifts amounts that need not be repaid.

WISE COUNSEL

Ultimately the Hansens had their first meeting with the financial counselor. It was not easy for Jack. He had done well and his strong ego had always kept him from meeting with any counselor, much less a financial advisor. Now he was forced to face someone and admit that he had not been successful in *every* aspect of his life.

Jack and Paula were not unlike most Yuppies, a term given in the 1980s to describe upwardly mobile professionals who wanted to advance in their careers, work hard, and enjoy all that, life had to offer. In many cases today, the Yuppies are married and find that in order to provide for their children's education, they must be willing to sacrifice some of life's comforts and pleasures. Eventually the Hansens were faced with that same decision.

The financial crisis the Hansens faced is very common for families without a proper budget to guide their expenditures. In fact, nearly 60 percent of all failed marriages fail because of "spending overload." Fortunately, the certified financial planner the Hansens chose to assist them, Michael Bainbridge, soon became a trusted advisor through their weekly meetings.

"There were times when I just wanted to . . . " Jack's lip began to quiver as he choked back his emotions. "Well, the pressure was so bad, there were times when I just wanted to give up!" Paula sat quietly and looked away as she tried to hold back tears. For a moment, the only sound in the room was the whisper sound from the air conditioner.

Then Michael responded, "I understand. When finances get a stranglehold on your marriage, they become a catalyst for placing you and your family into bondage. At that point, everything seems to fall apart."

"I thought I could handle it on my own," admitted Jack. "When business was good and we received a big bonus, I even bought a cabin cruiser. I suppose my biggest problem was that I kept up the spending even during the slow times. If I didn't have it, I'd charge it. I guess you would say I was out of control."

Over the next few months, Michael worked with both Paula and Jack in developing a spending plan that included trading their expensive luxury cars for mid-size automobiles, selling their club membership and their boat, and buying a smaller four-bedroom home. Having once been caught in the credit card "minimum payment trap," they retained only one card and promptly paid the balance in full each time they received a monthly statement.

"I don't understand. You always seem to know what is best for us. Where did you learn so much about finances?" Paula asked Michael one day.

Michael grinned as he humbly considered the question. "It's not my wisdom, but God's," he acknowledged. He then went on to explain the source of his knowledge concerning finances and told them how he had memorized the first ten verses of Proverbs chapter 10. "I frequently have to remind myself that it is God who gives wisdom and knowledge and understanding."

Michael then shared from the book of Romans in the Bible and told them how they too could have a personal relationship with God through His Son, Jesus Christ. As Paula and Jack listened to Michael, it seemed that each one began to realize that they had focused on the wrong things for years. An interest in deeper needs for themselves and their family eventually would lead them to return to church, something they had missed since their youth.

With the exception of their home mortgage, the lifestyle changes made by the Hansens would eventually allow them to become debt free. Jack slowly began his spiritual search, and they joined a Bible teaching church near their new home. Soon their marriage began to prosper. Financial wealth no longer remained their life's goal.

Over a period of time, Michael helped Jack invest some of his income and the profit he made on the sale of his club membership into a no-load mutual fund, which eventually generated a sizable return for his portfolio.

As a financial planner, Michael was also able to direct Emily to several reputable scholarship search organizations.

COLLEGE GRANTS BY THE STATES

"But what about grants from the state since I'm going to attend our state university?" asked Emily.

"State grants are not just for those who attend state-sponsored colleges," explained Michael. "Students often attend private schools and qualify for the grants. And some states even allow students to attend a college or university across the country."

Many state governments provide special grants for students attending a college or university within the state. In some cases, the grant money is labeled a "tuition equalization grant" and is available to offset higher tuition costs at private schools versus the state-supported colleges.

In other cases, the funds may be tied directly to the talent needs of the state. If, for example, a state is in need of nurses, medical technicians, math or science teachers, it may allow an undergraduate student to borrow from the state grant funds. Providing the student is employed in that field and that state for a certain number of years following graduation (usually one year for every year they borrow), the funds are not repayable. However, if the student leaves the state or the field of study, the remaining loan balance must be repaid with interest. This is known as a service-cancelable loan. Several kinds of service-cancelable loans, with their conditions for forgiving the loan balance, are discussed in detail in chapter 6.

Not every state has a service-cancelable program like the one described above. See appendix 6 for a complete listing of the state offices that administer special funding programs.

"Years ago, there were no Pell Grants, no Supplemental Grants, not even state grants," said Michael. "Students would get jobs doing just about anything to help make it through every semester. For example, let me tell you about my mother when she went to college.

"In 1953, my mother said good-bye to her parents' farm and headed for McPherson College in the adjoining state of Kansas. She and my grandparents had saved just enough to get her to school and pay for her first year. And my grandfather paid five dollars for a big, ole wooden trunk. Then they packed it with clothes made from material they found on clearance at the local dry goods store, and off she went to college."

Emily listened intently as Michael reminisced. She knew the financial advisor had a lesson here, but actually, she liked thinking about the older, simpler days. She leaned forward as Michael continued. "It wasn't long before she had a job as the campus editor for the school newspaper. The problem was that she wasn't paid, but she said she learned a lot and it made being away from home a little easier. Each summer she would return home and work for a large mailing house in central Iowa, typing thousands of names and addresses onto envelopes with an old manual typewriter. Because she learned the proofreading symbols in her editing class, she was eventually hired by the publisher of a daily newspaper in Iowa to help in the editorial department.

"Her jobs were not only interesting, but they paid for over half of her tuition, room, and board. Fortunately, my grandparents saved and scrimped for years and sent her a small allowance every month that she used for her expenses. In the mornings, she often walked about a mile and a half into downtown McPherson where she bought day-old rolls from the bakery and oranges from the grocery store. She ate breakfast in her dorm room instead of spending money in the cafeteria."

Michael described how his mother became editor in chief of the school newspaper and was even paid seventy-five cents per hour to write feature stories for the school. She kept a tight budget and always looked for other income sources.

"She told me she used to write all her expenditures down on a tablet and only allowed herself a dollar a day for food. She also did outside baby-sitting at fifty cents per hour and housecleaning and washing windows at sixty-five cents per hour to help meet expenses. It really is true, Emily; it's not how much you have, but how you manage it."

"But what about scholarships? Did your mother ever receive anything like that?" Emily asked.

"No, she never received any kind of gift grant or scholarship," said Michael. "But she was happy and graduated without debt. I guess you could say her grant was what she took away in blessings.

"I remember one of my classmates who had to make a lot of sacrifices in order to attend Pharmacy College. To avoid huge sums of student loans, he and his wife moved into the basement of his mother-in-law's house," explained Michael. "He then commuted every day for five years to the campus, some forty miles away. Eventually he was able to purchase a Ford van, and for a small fee, began to shuttle other students back and forth to the university, which helped cover his car payment and gasoline expenses.

"His wife worked almost full-time while taking care of their two little boys born during those college years. That, along with his part-time work and the GI Bill, enabled him to graduate with very little debt.

"Working at college is nothing to be ashamed of. Remember, it's not how much money you have at school, but how you manage what you do have," Michael reminded her.

Emily listened carefully and thought, *I sure hope I can graduate without a lot of debt.*

"Even though you're only a junior, Emily, it's never too early to begin looking for scholarships," Michael told her. "In fact, we'll set aside a special meeting just to go over all the details concerning college scholarships."

THE FEDERAL WORK-STUDY PROGRAM

The following year, Jack Hansen completed the financial aid request forms required for Emily and then, at the urging of Michael, made an appointment with the college financial aid administrator. While there, Emily learned that she did not qualify for the Federal Work-Study program as she had hoped.

"Based on your overall EFC, Emily, I cannot get you into the work-study program, but I will help you find work off campus," said the administrator.

However, many students will qualify for the federal work-study program, a campus-based program that can help them complete college with the least amount of student loans. Many students employed through the work-study program work right on campus, requiring little or no transportation time or expense. In addition, the program is administered through the financial aid department. Therefore, the money earned is neither taxed nor counted as income when the student reapplies.

The work-study jobs at most colleges are anything but boring. A student may be called upon to assist a scientist doing research at the college, work in the admissions office doing clerical work while greeting incoming high school students, work in the college library, or even help in the alumni office calling former students.

Once classes begin, students may work up to fifteen hours per week at minimum wage or better. College administrators like the plan because the school pays only half of the cost; the federal government picks up the balance. It's a 'win-win' for everyone.

Emily and her dad were disappointed that she did not qualify for a work-study position, but inquisitive about other part-time jobs on or off campus. "I know of several off-campus jobs that you may be interested in, Emily," said the administrator. "In fact, I have one in particular in mind that might even tie in with your field of study. I'll make a phone call right now for you."

The wise student keeps her eyes open for available positions and makes her interest known to the work-study coordinator. That's what Emily did; she was excited by the prospect of working on campus. "I really think I can learn a lot just by working here at the college," she told her dad. And when she got the position, she called Mr. Bainbridge.

"I'm very happy for you, Emily," said Michael. "You'll do great at college. Just keep your grades up and work hard and you'll be blessed in the long run. I received my best grades in college when I was working the greatest number of hours," added Michael. "Because of that, I always encourage students to find employment at college, whether through Uncle Sam's Work-Study program or directly on their own."

Indeed, the Federal Work-Study program, or any combination of work-study, offers valuable experience in a local work setting. It can be a valuable ally in a complete funding plan for college, especially when coupled with grants or scholarships. And there are many scholarships for which the student may qualify, as we will see in the next chapter.

chapter four

SCHOLARSHIP PROGRAMS

I t's never too early to begin looking for scholarships," Michael Bainbridge told Emily Hansen when she was a junior in high school. During the previous year, Michael had become a close friend while working with Emily's parents as their financial planner.

"I have heard of students waiting until they're ready to graduate from high school to start looking for financial aid. The problem is, once you find a scholarship source, it may take months before you're sent an application and then another six or eight months before any awards are handed out. Begin by looking through all the scholarship and college money books you find in the library," Michael advised.

Spending several hours looking through the maze of college financial aid books in the local library gave Emily firsthand knowledge concerning the private funds that were available. It also provided Emily an opportunity to rethink her decision about going to college and what course of study she would pursue.

During this period, Emily became interested in becoming a registered nurse. She was also very excited to find a great number of scholarships available just for nursing. For instance, she learned the American Legion sponsored the Eight & Forty Nursing Scholarships. Recipients had to enroll in a course of study to become registered nurses, specifically seeking a bachelor's or master's degree in the lung and respiratory field. The organization provides twenty-two scholarships annually worth $2,500.[1]

Emily's high school guidance counselor also suggested that she make a special effort to check with her church and her father's employer for other potential scholarships. This prompted Emily to ask about the college alumni association of the schools she was considering. Much to her surprise, the alumni group of one of the schools offered a sizable scholarship every year to a needy student. She heard about one student who applied for the scholarship after her freshman year of college and was granted a full tuition award for her second year based primarily on her first-year grades.

LOOKING FOR SCHOLARSHIPS LOCALLY AND ON THE INTERNET

Students seeking scholarships should look first in their own city or state before engaging in national competition. Many organizations such as the Elks Club, Kiwanis, Jaycees, Lions Club, American Legion, YMCA, 4-H and the U.S. Chamber of Commerce provide scholarships to local members or family members. In addition, there may be scholarships available from a local union group or foundation or from a particular company within the community.

A student who worked every afternoon as part of a student release program was entered into a community scholarship competition by her high school marketing teacher. Much to the girl's surprise, she was presented with a college scholarship worth several hundred dollars at an awards banquet sponsored by the local chamber of commerce.

"Don't forget to check out the information highway," commented Michael. "Because their costs are offset by advertising revenues, many of the scholarship search groups on the Internet are able to offer their services absolutely free, and some even provide frequent E-mail updates."

As Emily began searching for college finances on the Internet, Michael cautioned her to use discretion while surfing through multiple web sites. One search firm will provide a complete scholarship search for only $5.00. For a listing of more than one dozen web sites that offer scholarship and financial aid information for free or a nominal fee, including the $5.00 search service, see appendix 7.

TWO GREAT SCHOLARSHIP MYTHS

Charlotte Thomas, career and education editor for Peterson's, a publisher specializing in career and college books, put together a list of scholarship myths. The number one myth she cited was one Michael warned Emily about: "Billions" of scholarship dollars go unclaimed each year. Thomas affectionately calls this "the mother of all myths" and one that is frequently immortalized by the media.[2]

Unfortunately, every year many people believe the bogus story and are lured into spending hundreds of dollars with companies who promise to do all the required paperwork or guarantee at least $1,000 in financial aid or your money back. According to the College Board, some three hundred thousand people are cheated every year by scholarship scams despite efforts by the Federal Trade Commission to shut down the scam artists.[3]

The Federal Trade Commission notes that families may also fall prey to verbal claims, such as: "You can't get this information anywhere else;" "I just need your credit card or bank account number to hold the scholarship;" "You have been selected by a national foundation to receive a scholarship;" "You're a finalist in a scholarship contest;" "The money has already been reserved for you;" "Listen to what others are saying about us;" or "Billions in scholarship funds go unused every year."

Another myth often held by students is that the competition is too stiff. Thomas points out that scholarship contests are not just for valedictorians, but are open to every student willing to diligently seek out the scholarships.

HOW COLLEGES ARE HELPING

Most colleges and their financial aid administrators know about the struggles parents face in funding their children's education. They know the impact of ongoing increases in tuition and room-and-board costs. And they are responding. The amount of institutional aid offered annually by the colleges and universities is on the increase.

Complete and Partial Scholarships

A few colleges even offer complete scholarships for four years. For example, Rhodes College in Memphis, Tennessee, considers two high school seniors every year for one of their prestigious Walter D. Bellingrath or J. R. Hyde Scholarships, each worth the full cost of tuition, fees, and room and board. Candidates must be nominated by their high school guidance counselor, principal, headmaster, an alumnus, or trustee and submit their application for admission by January 15.

Those not qualifying for the Bellingrath or Hyde scholarships are automatically considered for over a hundred other Rhodes scholarships based solely on the candidate's academic record, leadership, character, and personal achievements. Some do include five Morse four-year scholarships awards worth a total of about $77,000, seventeen Cambridge Scholarships worth $58,000, and forty-eight University Scholarships valued at $38,000. Furthermore, the school offers more than sixty other scholarship awards each year of various amounts.

In addition, schools sometimes prepare special financial packages as they compete for top students, including large merit scholarships. Although most colleges and universities are reluctant to offer straight discounts to incoming students struggling with sticker shock, they are able to offset the high costs and be competitive by providing grant aid. Essentially, a student grant is based either on need like the Pell Grant, or on merit such as academic or athletic scholarships. Neither has to be repaid. One student received a "Leadership Scholarship" after it was learned that her parents could not afford the tuition at a private Christian school. The scholarship was not a published award, but offered as part of their overall recruitment effort. Since the student did not have to repay the funds, the award had the same attributes as a student grant.

No matter how the finances are distributed or what they are called, whether a discount, grant, or scholarship, the award still serves to minimize student debt.

Home-Schooled Students Welcomed

It is not uncommon for colleges to use financial aid as a recruiting tool and offer merit scholarships to those students with elevated SAT and ACT scores, special athletic abilities, or those recommended by people of very high authority or reputation. That aid is available regardless of where they have been schooled. That includes students schooled at home. While some states are slow in recognizing and accepting home-schoolers on a par with other high school graduates, once the college admissions committee accepts the student, the process of applying for financial aid is the same. Home-schooled students submit the same forms, face the same methodology in determining need, and have the same test scores evaluated. Significantly, they find that the same grants, scholarships, and loans are readily available.

Nationally, every college and university will evaluate students who have completed the home-education curriculum on three factors: demonstrated need, scholastic achievement, and their ability to negotiate. Negotiations can often land a tuition reduction based solely on documentation and how the school perceives the student at the time of application.

About "Negotiations"

Negotiations may become an ongoing way of life for every student in the future. One large national university invites students to notify the school if a better financial aid package is offered from another college. In some cases, the university will match the other award or even increase it.

Admission officers and financial aid staff, however, do not use the term "negotiate." In fact, even though many negotiate on a regular basis, most will not admit to it nor use the term in their discussions with students and parents.

Often colleges will assist students who have completed one or two years of classes and shown themselves diligent and capable. Students who performed well but not at the top in the college testing during their high school years (primarily SAT and ACT described in the next section) may find the college later rewarding their diligence.

Michael Bainbridge told Emily Hansen about Alison, a student enrolled in a southern university without qualifying for a scholarship because her highest SAT was 1140. Although Alison realized the importance of the SAT (Scholastic Assessment Test), she did not fully prepare for it and her performance was average.

"Alison was in her junior year in college," Michael continued, "and by that time, directly involved in her major. While she had always done well academically, it was during her junior year that the dean of the department noticed her continual 4.0 average every quarter. And it was the dean who came forward and offered her a full tuition scholarship for her senior year and then again for her fifth year of college."

"Was that a scholarship from the financial aid office?" asked Emily.

"No; the scholarship from the department head was not through the financial aid office although they were the ones who posted the award," responded Michael. "It was actually from a private donor who sent money to the university each year and requested that it be specifically given to a student excelling in that particular field of study."

"What was she studying?" asked Emily.

"She was studying to be a registered dietitian, and I understand she is now in her second year of graduate school to complete her studies," answered Michael.

Most universities and some smaller schools have a growing number of private donors who direct their contribution to a particular department or college within the university. While this money flows through the financial aid office, it is awarded to those students who meet or exceed all expectations by department heads or even the academic dean.

"This was not an isolated case, Emily. Many students who do not qualify for a scholarship as a new student will later receive an academic scholarship if, and that's a big if, they work hard and show great promise. There is a lot of money for academically motivated students," concluded Michael.

SCHOLARSHIPS FROM THE ACADEMIC TESTING SERVICES

The college testing services perform a great service for colleges and students alike. Not only do they measure academic progress and potential, they can reward students who score high on the test. Parents should encourage their children to take the PSAT (Preliminary Scholastic Assessment Test) during their junior year of high school. Those who score high on the PSAT may receive worthy recognition as a winner of one of the seven thousand prestigious National Merit Scholarships. Other participants may earn recognition as a National Merit semifinalist. Although semifinalists do not receive scholarships, their achievement looks notable on a college application. For more information, write the nonprofit National Merit Scholarship Corporation, 1560 Sherman Avenue, Suite 200, Evanston, Illinois 60201.

Scholarships may also be awarded based on the SAT or the ACT (American College Testing Assessment), although the two tests are entirely different. Some educators believe that the SAT is more of an "aptitude" test to evaluate a student's ability to do college-level work, while the ACT is more of an "achievement" test, evaluating the skills already mastered. Both tests may be taken each year beginning in the seventh grade to help parents and teachers assess a student's overall proficiency every year.

Countless students are not aware of the heavy national competition with students receiving concentrated exam preparation from qualified tutors for both tests. Because of the overwhelming acceptance of the national testing programs for academic scholarships and admission into the best schools, all students seeking merit-based awards should consider tutorial assistance prior to their final testing date, whether schooled at home or in a public or private high school. Remember, students whose test scores are mediocre (in the average percentile) typically receive most of their financial aid in the form of high-cost student loans.

As noted in chapter 1, the Princeton Review offers courses to help students to maximize their PSAT, SAT, SAT II, or ACT scores. This nationally recognized organization assists students in overall preparation, often advancing students well over 100 points between their junior and senior testing dates. The group also publishes the average test scores for incoming students at hundreds of colleges and universities across the country for comparative purposes.[4]

Meanwhile, the Kaplan Educational Center at www1.kaplan.com publishes books on standardized testing preparation. See your local bookstore or the above web site. The firm also maintains their own links to information on nursing, law school, medicine, accounting, and other tutorial aids plus tips in budgeting, ways to save money while at college, and how to avoid problems with credit cards.

IMPROVING SCHOLARSHIP CHANCES

In addition to completing academic testing programs such as the PSAT, SAT, and ACT, students increase their scholarship potential by completing advanced placement classes. The AP classes are college-level courses available to high school students in twenty subjects, with two new subjects to be added by 2002. (Not every subject is available in every school.)

Advanced placement classes are important for several reasons. As noted in chapter 1, college admissions committees view students who have passed several AP classes very favorably. In addition, there are overall cost savings. Students who complete the AP course and then take the optional Advanced Placement Examination on the subject, scoring at least three (out of five) on the exam may earn college credits, which can save thousands of dollars. (Most schools offer such courses, which have a more rigorous curriculum than the average version of the course.) Further, there are over fourteen hundred colleges and universities in America that will issue sophomore standing to an incoming student who has successfully passed the number of advanced placement classes required by the institution.

More significantly, AP classes can benefit the student's grade point average, a key component in the formula of many scholarships. Advanced Placement classes enable students to earn a grade higher than their overall scores. In other words, a student who earns a B in an advanced placement class scores a 4.0, whereas a grade of A is posted as a 5.0.

NOTEWORTHY SCHOLARSHIPS

Most parents are interested in the Hope Scholarship and wonder if their prospective college student will qualify. Actually, the Hope Scholarship is not really a scholarship; it would be better named the Hope program. It's an income tax credit that some parents can receive during their student's first two years of college. The Hope is a federal program that allows a tax credit of $1,500 per year for two years. Based on the parents' income, the mother and father will be eligible for a tax credit equal to 100 percent of the first $1,000 of tuition and 50 percent of the second $1,000 of tuition for their student's freshman and sophomore years. For detailed information on tax credits, see appendix 8.

One true scholarship that offers up to $1,500 a year is the Robert C. Byrd Honors Scholarship. Unlike the Hope program, the $1,500 is granted each year for four years. With the Byrd Scholarship, it doesn't matter where the student attends school. He can use the money for any college or university in the United States. However, the student must apply before graduating from high school.

The Robert C. Byrd Honors Scholarship, named after the former Senate majority leader, is a federally financed grant funded by taxpayer dollars and administered by state officials. Unlike the Federal Pell Grant and the Federal Supplemental Educational Opportunity Grant, the Byrd Scholarship is not based on financial need. The total number of scholarships is determined by federal appropriations per congressional district. A complete listing of state offices administering the special Byrd scholarship is found in appendix 9.

Another nationwide scholarship of note that offers a larger cash award is the Harry S. Truman Scholarship, given to college students at the end of their junior year who plan to pursue graduate studies. Nominees must show a desire and aptitude to pursue careers in government or elsewhere in public service and wish to attend graduate and professional school to help prepare for their careers. "Truman Scholars participate in leadership development programs and have special opportunities for internships and employment with the federal government," the foundation reports.

Truman scholars—almost eighty in the year 2000—are awarded a $3,000 scholarship for their senior year and an additional $13,500 per year as they continue a two-year master's program, or an additional $9,000 per year if they enroll in a three-year master's program. Thus Truman scholars receive $27,000 for their graduate studies, for a total of $30,000 toward the cost of their undergraduate and graduate education. The Truman Scholarship Foundation honors one student per state, plus one each in the District of Columbia, Puerto Rico, or the "Islands" (composed of Guam, the Virgin Islands, American Samoa, and Northern Mariana Islands). Up to thirty additional at-large scholars are also selected.

Although Truman scholars have come from such traditional fields as economics, education, government, history, international relations law, public administration, and public health, other fields have been represented, including agriculture, biology, engineering, physical and social science, and technology policy. For more information, students can visit the Harry S. Truman Scholarship Foundation web site at www.truman.gov.

COMPLETING SCHOLARSHIP APPLICATIONS AND ESSAYS

Some Dos and Don'ts

No matter what scholarship you apply for, there are a few dos and don'ts you need to know. First and foremost, as a student, apply on time. You may even wish to keep a file on each scholarship with their address, the application deadline, and the progress on each item. When possible, send your application in two or three weeks before the deadline. Many students wait until the last minute, and then because they feel pressured, they rush through their application and essay and end up making a very poor impression on the scholarship review committee.

Michael relayed those dos and don'ts to Emily, who felt her busy schedule would leave little time to compose several essays. "Am I required to write an essay for every scholarship?" asked Emily, rather concerned.

Writing the Essay

"Many scholarship applications and even admissions applications require an essay, the tougher the better," Michael emphasized. "It helps to cut down on the competition. Some people consider the essay the most important part of the application."

In *Do It Write*, G. Gary Ripple, the admissions director at Lafayette College, echoes the importance of writing an effective essay. "It's without question, the most difficult and the most important element over which you have control in the admissions process. A well-written essay will differentiate the truly exciting student from the merely good one, and tip the scale in favor of the former."[5] See appendix 10 for some practical tips on essay writing.

"Some applications do not require an essay but rather a long explicatory reason of why you should receive the award. You need to know why and be able to put your answer down in a very clear and thought-provoking manner," added Michael. "Those who read all the applications look for expressed ambitions and want to know what makes you different from every other applicant.

"You may need to send out as many as twenty or thirty applications. Learn who is sponsoring the scholarship, look them up on the Internet or in a library, and then customize your essay to fit *their* interests. The more you know about the organization, the better your chances of winning the award.

"Don't brag about yourself," Michael went on, "but emphasize your achievements and your leadership skills. Just be who you are, Emily, and present your essay in a logical, well-planned manner. And, oh, yes, throw away your thesaurus and buy a copy of *The Elements of Style* by William Strunk and E. B. White.

"The key is to write something that's original, something about you that will compel the reader to continue reading your essay. Both scholarship committees and admissions committees want to understand what motivates you. You may want to write about your extracurricular activities and volunteer work and share your personal feelings concerning how a particular experience affected you and what you learned from the experience.

"Recently I noted that one admissions director said he would rather read why a particular book was important to you than hear about the book itself. He then went on to say he would rather read about a conversation you had with someone on a trip than to read the details of the trip.

"Finally, don't forget the five W's of journalistic writing: who, what, why, when, and where. When you have all five W's covered, you can simply stop writing. I like to remind students of something I learned in a college speech class," Michael chuckled. "I had a cranky old professor who always told us to prepare our audience in our opening comments. In other words, 'Set the stage with your introduction,' he'd say. He would grumble and mumble and often repeat himself while telling us not to do the same. 'And then in conclusion,' he'd go on, 'don't bore them with what you've just told them; make your close and quit.'

"One more thing," Michael continued, "be sure your essay and the entire scholarship application is neat. Ask your parents and maybe even some of your teachers to proofread it. Just in case you make a mistake, you may want to photocopy the application and fill out a few draft copies before completing the official form.

"Keep in mind, Emily, that some merit-based scholarships may want you to include copies of your high school transcript, your class ranking, and your national test scores along with the letters of recommendation. You may also wish to send a short cover letter thanking them for considering you for their scholarship award," commented Michael.

"Grades are very important, Emily, and your test scores must be exceptional."

The Role of School and Community Activities

Students can improve chances for some scholarships by showing leadership potential and involvement in school and community activities. Not every student will be in the top 10 percent of the class, but everyone can be involved in extracurricular activities. That's important too when you're applying for a scholarship.

Paula and Jack Hansen always encouraged Emily and her sister, Sara, to be involved in their junior high and high school music programs. Emily was also involved in the local Habitat for Humanity building program. "It's so cool," said Emily. "Some of the people we help would never be able to get a house, *ever*," she excitedly blurted out one day.

Twice a month, Emily's mother, Paula, would help out as a volunteer at one of the health clinics in the city. When Emily wasn't swinging a hammer or sawing boards, she would also volunteer at the clinic. "I'm always busy on Saturdays," Emily commented. "It's OK, though. I'd rather be busy for a worthwhile cause than just hanging out at the mall."

As a result of her continued community service, Emily received the President's Student Service Scholarship based on her high school principal's recommendation. The $1,000 annual scholarship is awarded to one junior or senior in each high school that exemplifies outstanding conduct and leadership through their community service work. For more information, log on to www.cns.gov.

SCHOLARSHIPS FROM CORPORATE AMERICA

Many scholarships are sponsored by some of America's largest and most respected entrepreneurs. For example, Atlanta-based Chick-fil-A Corporation awards hundreds of $1,000 Leadership Scholarships every year to their brightest young employees. In addition, the top twenty-five recipients also receive the S. Truett Cathy Award of $1,000. Chick-fil-A also is a partner with Berry College in

Rome, Georgia, providing an impressive $24,000 each year to one new student for the WinShape scholarship.

The Duracell/NSTA Invention Challenge invites students to design and build working devices powered by Duracell batteries. Administered by the National Science Teachers Association, the competition is open to individuals or teams of two in grades six through twelve. Altogether, there are one hundred winners in the Duracell/NSTA Scholarship Challenge: fifty for grades six through nine and fifty for grades ten through twelve. Two first-place winners each receive a $20,000 savings bond; four second-place winners, a $10,000 savings bond; awards range to a $500 savings bond granted to sixty fifth-place winners. Thousands of dollars are also presented to the teachers of the winners.

The Coca-Cola Scholars Program is open to all high school seniors in the United States. Every year, fifty students are recognized as National Scholars and each receives a $20,000 award for college. An additional two hundred Regional Scholars receive a $4,000 award. The Coca-Cola Foundation also provides a Hispanic Scholarship Fund and a "First to Go" scholarship designed for students who are the first in their family to attend college.[6]

The Siemens Westinghouse Science and Technology Competition is a national competition for independent research completed in high school. The top prize is $120,000. There are also six individual regional winners of $20,000 each (or $30,000 if divided among two or three team members).

The program is designed to promote and encourage students to undertake individual or team research projects in science, math, and technology, and may include submissions in math and the biological and physical sciences. Specific information is found at www.siemens-foundation.org.

The National Academy of American Scholars (NAAS) sponsors the Easley National Scholarships for high school seniors. The only qualifications are that the applicants are high school seniors, U.S. residents, and have been accepted into an accredited four-year academic program.

NAAS also sponsors the National NAAS-II Scholarship for college freshman. Applicants must be U.S. citizens currently enrolled as college freshmen in an accredited college or university. Scholarships range from four-year renewable awards of $10,000, $6,000, and $4,000 to smaller scholarships and cash awards. Interested students may log on to www.naas.org for details.

Most fraternal organizations also offer scholarships. For instance, the National Foundation for the Elks annually awards four-year scholarships to five hundred of the top students in the nation. Appropriately named the "Most Valuable Student" competition, the awards range from $1,000 per year to $7,500 per year for the four-year period. Applicants need to be in the top 5 percent of their class, have leadership qualities, and indicate financial need. Students are not required to be a member or related to a member, but must be recommended by a local Elks Club.

EMILY'S EDUCATION

The research and preparation by the Hansens brought Emily several types of financial assistance. In addition to the merit scholarship received from the university as a result of her high school transcript and SAT scores, Emily also qualified for two outside awards based on her application essays.

During her four years of training to become a registered nurse, Emily held several jobs. Emily's work ethic also inspired and encouraged all who knew her. Working not only freed her from accepting excessive student loans, it also helped her parents during their most difficult times of financial bondage. Emily graduated debt free, ready to focus on helping others, as an R.N., as she had dreamed since high school.

NOTES

1. To learn more about the Eight & Forty Scholarship and other scholarships from the American Legion, students should send $3 to American Legion Headquarters, P.O. Box 1055, Indianapolis, Indiana 46206 and request the current edition of *Need a Lift*.
2. Ms. Thomas' article is found on the Internet at the Peterson's web site, at www.petersons.com/resources/myths.html; accessed on 25 February 2000.
3. Cited on the Internet at www.collegeboard.org/gp/hartman/html/apr2.html; accessed on 13 March 2000.
4. The Princeton Review can be found on the web by going to www.review.com or calling 800-2REVIEW.
5. G. Gary Ripple, *Do It Write*, 5th ed. (Alexandria, Va.: Octameron Associates, 1999), 11.
6. For more information on the WinShape award, call 800-448-6955. For information on Duracell/NSTA Invention Challenge, call or write the challenge at Duracell/NSTA Invention Challenge, 1840 Wilson Blvd., Arlington, VA 22201, 888-255-4242 or find them on the Internet at www.nsta.org/programs/duracell/.(Deadline is early January.) For information on the Coca-Cola Scholars Program, its Hispanic Scholarship Fund, and the First to Go scholarship, go to the Internet web site at www.coca-colacompany.com.

chapter five

ATHLETIC SCHOLARSHIPS

Between her sophomore and junior years in high school, Megan, Bill Forsyth's younger daughter, enrolled in a lifeguard-training program sponsored by the YMCA. This gave Megan something to do during the summer months when she was not playing soccer for her high school.

As expected, Megan did very well in the training class and was hired by a local pool management company to serve at one of the community pools. Nevertheless, Megan's interest was always in playing soccer.

"I'd love to play soccer at college, but there are so few teams," she said one day, feeling rather discouraged.

The high school coach had watched Megan play soccer when she was still in middle school. It seemed obvious to everyone that someday she would be an outstanding player on the high school varsity team. She liked to play forward and when she was only twelve years old, her coach persuaded her to use her left foot to shoot goals. "Keepers are seldom ready for left-footed kickers," said her coach. "Shoot with your left; shoot with your left!" he would shout.

As a result of her coach's consistent encouragement and Megan's persistent practice, she became very proficient with her left foot and scored several goals in every game.

Now as a forward for her high school team, Megan had a solid game. One day Megan and her close friend, Natasha, met with the high school athletic director,

Mr. Jenkins, and asked him about scholarships for college.

"Everyone says there are a lot of scholarships, but they all go to the football or basketball guys," said Natasha. "Is that true, Mr. Jenkins? Do you think I could get a scholarship to play volleyball?"

"It's not true that all the money goes to the football and basketball players," responded Mr. Jenkins, "and yes, Natasha, you may well qualify for a volleyball scholarship.

"Of course, a great amount of the money does go to the college basketball and football athletes. The reason is because those sports help provide the largest amount of revenues—revenues needed for new buildings, computer labs, and maybe even a new stadium. In a way, successful college football and basketball programs help pay for other programs. Therefore, colleges and universities recruit the best players using scholarships as a recruiting tool."

Jenkins mentioned two major athletic associations, the National Collegiate Athletic Association (NCAA) and the National Association of Intercollegiate Athletics (NAIA), which sanction the sports activities and determine how much and how many scholarships schools can award. But then he offered Natasha and Megan hope.

"There are many college sports besides football and basketball where men and women can qualify for a scholarships. In fact, the NCAA watches over twenty-two different sports altogether, and that includes college-level volleyball.

"The NAIA is also very strong among smaller colleges and universities. If you attend one of their schools, you could receive a scholarship whether you excel in field hockey or lacrosse, cross-country or rowing," Mr. Jenkins added. "The point is, there are thousands of scholarship opportunities out there for the top athletes, regardless of the sport. Furthermore, there is the NCAA Women's Enhancement Program specifically for young women like Megan and you who want to compete in college sports and later work with intercollegiate athletes."

SPECIFIC SCHOLARSHIPS FOR STUDENT ATHLETES

"One very intriguing scholarship you need to check on, Natasha, is the NCAA Minority Program," said Mr. Jenkins. "As an African-American, you may qualify for that scholarship. Just get on the Internet and go to the NCAA web page at www.ncaa.org.

"Make sure you both stay in touch and register with the NCAA," Mr. Jenkins continued. "In order for you to be eligible to play, you must register and be certified by the association's initial-eligibility clearinghouse, and that includes sending your national test scores. The registration fee is only eighteen dollars. If you're not sure about what to do, see your guidance counselor or call the athletic association at 319-337-1492. You can also get in touch with the NAIA online at www.naia.org."

As the girls were leaving his office, Mr. Jenkins told them about a postgraduate scholarship sponsored by the NCAA that recognizes student-athletes who excelled in both sports and academics during their college career. "Every year approximately one hundred fifty athletes receive a $5,000 award to attend graduate school and only about a third of those winners are football and basketball players," added Mr. Jenkins.

"That's what I want to do," Natasha blurted out.

"As a final note," Mr. Jenkins interjected, "ask your volleyball coach to give you some ideas about inviting different college coaches here to see you play. It's important for coaches to see you play in person whenever possible. If the school is too far away or the coach is unable to travel here, you might try taking your game to her. For example, some parents put together a composite video to show the coaches. Hey, maybe your dad can shoot a video and call it, 'The Best of Natasha,'" he said with a big smile.

Everyone laughed, and their meeting encouraged both Megan and Natasha.

ABOUT COLLEGIATE RECRUITING OF ATHLETES

There are specific rules that govern students and coaches when recruited to play a particular sport for a college or university. Recruiters have guidelines and limitations when it comes to offering financial aid and making promises. Be wary of coaches and other recruiters offering extra money before or after enrolling at their school. Check out the web site www.ncaa.org/eligibility/cbsa for a review of the rules under Division I Recruiting.

In addition, there are several national recruiting organizations that promise top-flight results for college-bound student-athletes; they do charge a fee for their services. Parents and students should investigate each organization prior to making any investment. One such organization is the National Recruiting Network at www.info@nationalrecruits.com that puts together a "game plan" for each student seeking athletic scholarships. Another recruiting firm at http://scoutingonline.8m.com promises to provide the athlete with exposure to two thousand colleges.

WHICH COLLEGE TO CHOOSE

One question that average, above-average, and gifted high school athletes must answer is this: "Should I seek a scholarship with a big athletic program with a successful ranked team, or should I go to a smaller athletic program with lesser funding, recognition, and success?" Some argue the big school with big athletic programs will give student-athletes better skills training in their position, a shot at major exposure and honor when they excel on the playing arena, court, or field, and a chance—even if a slim one—of making it professionally. Others say a small school gives you more individualized attention and the likelihood of more playing time.

Clearly, there are pros and cons for learning and playing sports in the NCAA, the NAIA, or the NCCAA—the National Christian College Athletic Association. Be careful of generalizations, however. Students from small schools, including small Christian schools,[1] can be spotted and go on to play in the pros, such as Christian Okoye of the NFL's Kansas City Chiefs (Azusa Pacific University), Sid Bream of Major League Baseball's Pittsburgh Pirates and Atlanta Braves (Liberty University), and Tim Belcher of the Anaheim Angels and Kansas City Royals (Olivet Nazarene University). And coaches at most major NCAA schools do care about their student-athletes' classroom performance.

There are many fundamental similarities among the three athletic associations, even if the NCAA gets almost all the television coverage and most of the newspaper reporting in the large metropolitan areas. Whether you enroll and play for an NCAA, NAIA, or NCCAA school, each member school will have a medical doctor either on staff or minutes away, ready to assist a student-athlete if hurt. Most schools have excellent coaches, including the smaller schools. And almost every school cares about the student-athlete's classroom performance; some try to help with tutoring and/or academic counseling. They know that most will not continue to a professional sports career, and that their students are here first and foremost to earn an academic degree; their sports ability is helping them earn scholarships to fulfill that primary goal. (Some advise a lighter academic load while the sport is in season. This, of course, can delay the graduation date, adding costs, but there are benefits to this approach.)

The high school student-athlete looking toward a scholarship and playing experience on the college level should select the school that best fits his or her athletic and academic abilities. Setting priorities, weighing each factor, doing research, and consulting high school coaches and academic counselors will help the student-athlete arrive at the right decision. Conversations with other student-athletes during campus visits, or with those who have already graduated, may also prove enlightening and beneficial.

EQUAL OPPORTUNITIES FOR MALE AND FEMALE STUDENT-ATHLETES

As she continued to look into scholarship opportunities for athletes, Megan soon learned about Title IX, which gives women athletes more opportunities for sports involvement by mandating equal number of programs for male and female athletes. In fact, while Megan was working as a lifeguard during the summer after high school graduation, she heard that the university she was planning to attend was going to hold tryouts for a new Division I soccer team—a new women's sport brought about by Title IX requirements. Suddenly, Megan let out a loud and joyful shout and then scrambled to find another guard to substitute for her while she attended the tryouts. The next day she grabbed a pillow and suitcase and announced, "I'll be back in a few days."

Despite the summer heat at the tryouts, Megan excelled, made the team, and did not return for two months. She was a walk-on; that is, she was not recruited but walked on the field and impressed the coach during tryouts. She was awarded an athletic scholarship from the university, plus an academic tutor if needed, and complete access to the sports medical staff.

Title IX helped Megan in two ways. It helped one university she liked to develop a sports team she loved, and it made scholarships available—including one that had Megan's name on it. The Title IX decision governing college athletics has been well received by many athletes. Other athletes, however, have been clearly hurt by the decision as their particular sport was eliminated in order to budget for women's athletics. In 1999, for instance, Miami (of Ohio) University ended three men's intercollegiate sports to make way for more women's teams.

Natasha made the "All State" volleyball team, and even before high school graduation, had already received three proposals to play women's volleyball at college. During her senior year, Natasha and her parents visited two of the three schools. Eventually Natasha decided on a West Coast university that offered her a "full ride" scholarship where she played for four years, graduating with honors.

Students who hope to play college athletics should begin planning as early as their high school freshman year. Each year the high school student should take specific steps, according to Jim and Mary Herb in their booklet, *In Search of the Athletic Scholarship*. They recommend, for instance, that during the sophomore year, students "continue striving for academic success, research NCAA academic requirements. . . . [and] stay active in Club Volleyball and High School Volleyball. . . . During the summer between the Sophomore and Junior years, prepare your athletic résumé."[2] They offer many more suggestions for the Sophomore year as well as the other three years in a time line appearing at the web address www.home.earthlink.net/~tfakehany/timeline.html.

Updated reference guides for student-athletes excelling in baseball, softball, soccer, and volleyball are available through Sport Source Publications (800-862-3092; the cost is $27.95 for each book plus shipping and handling) or on the Internet at www.thesportsource.com

Whether you're considering a big school or small school—or both—and whether your sport is soccer, volleyball, or one of more than a dozen sports found among the three major athletic associations (NAIA, NCAA, and NCCAA), partial to full scholarships are waiting to help you develop and enjoy your athletic skills while completing a college education.

NOTES

1. An excellent resource for information on intercollegiate sports offered among schools in the National Christian College Athletic Association (Division I through III) is chapter 9, "Christian College Athletics" in Dave Branon, *A Sports Fan's Guide to Christian Athletes and Sports Trivia* (Chicago: Moody, 2000). The chapter also lists NCCAA championships won by schools in sixteen sports during the 1980s and 1990s.
2. Jim and Mary Herb, *In Search of the Athletic Scholarship;* as cited in Tom Fakehany, "Timeline for College Athletic Scholarships," on the Internet at www.home.earthlink.net/~tfakehany/timeline.html, accessed on 4 January 2000. The article also tells readers how to obtain a copy of Jim Herb's article, "How to Write an Athletic Résumé."

chapter six

SERVICE-CANCELABLE LOANS: LOANS THAT BECOME GRANTS

I found it! I found it!" shouted Brian to his father coming in from the field. "I think I found a way I can go. Look at this!"

Brian had in his hand a fact sheet that told about a government program that was started years before as a means for students to borrow money for college and then settle the obligation through a service plan. The plan would forgive, or cancel, all or part of the student loan on the condition that the student works in a particular career for a number of years. With the loan balance being forgiven in whole or in part, the loan acts as a grant.

"What's all the excitement about, Brian?" asked Lester Johnson, Brian's father, as he brushed off some of the hay that was still clinging to his pants.

"This may be the way we can afford it, Dad. Look; it says that I can borrow some money but not have to pay it back. Well, I do have pay it back, but not with money. I mean, I just have to work to pay it back," Brian tried to explain.

Work was never a problem for Brian. Both he and his older brother, Blake, had worked early morning chores for years on the Johnson farm. Brian still remembered being awakened early every morning to milk the cows before leaving for school. *I'm sure glad Dad sold all those cows to a big dairy producer.* Brian chuckled at the thought.

"Settle down, Son," said Brian's father. "Now what is this you're talking about, some kind of government subsidy?"

"I don't know if that's what you call it, Dad, but it says here I can borrow with this Perkins deal and work only five years to pay back all the money. Maybe I could even work for the police department," said Brian with a big smile.

Lester Johnson was well versed on government subsidies. For years, he and his neighbors in Ohio had fought to keep the government out of the farming business, but to no avail. Eventually, he too accepted what he called a "government handout" when the crops on his small farm failed to produce as he had hoped. He didn't like it, but he knew it had kept him going in the lean years.

The Johnson farm was a low-yield producer, and Lester often thought about selling the acreage, but he had been unable to find a major corporation that was interested. Lester's wife, Gladys, started working in a nearby town, and her income helped to pay off some of their debts at the local farm implement store.

I suppose he'll be leaving the farm too, thought Lester as he pondered over the information Brian had showed him. Brian's older brother, Blake, had already vacated the farm. *That leaves only Susie, our twelve-year old, to take over.*

"Well, that just ain't gonna happen," Lester suddenly blurted out.

"What's not going to happen?" asked Brian.

"Oh nothin', Son. I was just thinkin' something about your sister. Never mind, never mind," Lester said.

"This here sounds pretty good to me, Brian, but are you sure you can pay it all back just doing police work in town?" asked Lester.

"It says I can, Dad, but it doesn't have to be in town. Why, maybe I could even get a job with the FBI. Wow, that would be cool!" added Brian.

Brian knew he didn't want to end up like his older brother. *He just works in that ole body shop every day and then hangs out at the pool hall with all his buddies every night. That's not for me,* thought Brian. *I want to do something and be somebody, or at least not waste my time playing pool.*

UNDERSTANDING THE PERKINS LOAN

Provisions of the Perkins Loan

The program that Brian had uncovered was not new. The federal Perkins Loan is one of the most sought-after financial aid programs available. It was especially exciting for Brian because of his interest in law enforcement. And, of course, it's available to every student, whether he lives on a farm in Peoria, a ranch in Boise, or a bungalow in Berkeley.

The Perkins Loan is a need-based loan funded by the government and administered by the colleges. Undergraduate students may borrow up to $4,000 per year to a maximum of $20,000. Graduate students may borrow an additional $20,000. Best of all, Uncle Sam pays the interest while the student is in school.

What makes the Perkins Loan so popular is the low interest rate of only 5 percent compared to a maximum of more than 8 percent for the Stafford Loan and 9 percent for the Parent Loan. The loan has a nine-month grace period after graduation, and allows the student up to ten years to complete the loan repayment. Furthermore, there is no loan origination fee, which saves the student an additional 4 percent. If a student were to borrow the maximum $40,000 available, the savings on the origination fees alone would be $1,600. For comparative loan repayment figures, see appendix 11.

Conditions for Canceling the Loan Balance

Like the Stafford Loan, the Federal Perkins Loan may be canceled for death or permanent and total disability. In addition, the Perkins Loan is also cancelable, in effect becoming a cash grant, if the borrower becomes:

- a full-time teacher (whether or not certified or licensed) or, under certain conditions, a teacher's aide in a public or private nonprofit elementary or secondary school system for math, science, foreign languages, bilingual education, special education (including teachers of infants, preschool, or youth with disabilities), or any other field of expertise where the state agency determines a shortage, or in a school system serving low-income students, typically for a period of five years. If teaching less than five years, the loan balance is forgiven at a set, prorated basis for each year.

- a full-time staff member in the educational part of a Head Start preschool program. In this field the cancellation rate is set at 15 percent per year for each year of employment, which would require a little more than six years of service for the loan to be fully canceled.

- a full-time licensed practical or registered nurse or a certified, registered, or licensed medical technician providing health care services in fields such as "therapy, dental hygiene, medical technology, or nutrition." The employment period for full cancellation of the loan is typically five years for this field and those that follow.

- a full-time law enforcement or corrections officer at the local, state, or federal level.

- a full-time employee at a public or private nonprofit child or family service agency, providing the services are directed to high-risk children (those under age twenty-one from low-income communities) or those at risk of abuse or neglect or who have been abused or neglected, have serious emotional, mental, or behavioral disturbances, reside in placements outside their homes, are involved in the juvenile justice system, and/or the families of the children.

- a full-time qualified professional provider of early intervention services in a public or private nonprofit program including special educators, speech and language pathologists and audiologists, occupational therapists, physical therapists, psychologists, social workers, nurses, and nutritionists.

Significantly, students must meet one other condition of eligibility. The student must apply for cancellation by filing the required forms at the school where the loan originated. School officials at the college or university where the loan originated determine whether the student is entitled to have any portion of the loan canceled, based on the federal guidelines noted above.

The Perkins Loan has made a major difference in many families. Consider two sisters who attended Auburn University several years ago; we'll call one Ann, the other Kay. Ann majored in communications; Kay in education. Based on parental income, both students qualified for a Federal Perkins Loan.

Ann graduated and soon began to live out a lifelong dream as a flight attendant for Delta Air Lines. After a nine-month grace period, her Perkins Loan became due and she dutifully paid the lender $50 each month year after year.

Her sister, on the other hand, graduated with a teaching credential that allowed her to work with students who were diagnosed with severe behavioral problems. Nine months after she graduated, Kay's Perkins Loan also became due, but since she chose to teach special education in private and public schools, her loan was handled in an entirely different way. The cancellation rate on her Perkins Loan agreement allowed for a reduction of 15 percent per year for the first two years, 20 percent per year for the next two years, and the balance for her fifth year. Because she stayed in special education for five years, 100 percent of her student loan was canceled, including all finance charges.

BRIAN'S STORY

Brian's interest in attending college and going into law enforcement was well received by everyone at their church, a small country church where members were very close and committed to one another. Both Gladys and Lester Johnson had grown up attending church every Sunday morning. Wednesday evenings many families would have dinner together prior to a Bible study. It was important to the Johnsons that each of their three children would have a saving knowledge of the Lord Jesus Christ. The Johnsons' two sons invited Christ into their lives one summer at a church camp, and Brian became very close to the pastor and his wife. In fact, they often referred to him as their "adopted son in the Lord."

In the past when someone left for college, it was very common for the church to provide a small scholarship for each semester. While most young men attended the state agricultural school, the pastor and deacons approved the same scholarship for Brian.

In the fall of his senior year in high school, Brian applied for acceptance to a private Christian college. After receiving his acceptance notice, Brian and his father filled out the FAFSA that determined Brian's expected family contribution and his eligibility for student financial aid.

Since the Johnson farm was also the family's prime residence, Lester Johnson did not have to report the value of the farm on the FAFSA. Based on family income, therefore, Brian did qualify for a Perkins Loan. The financial aid office reminded Brian that there was no guarantee that the loan would be forgiven unless he went into one of the occupations for which the loan is service cancelable. Brian was also eligible for the federal work-study, but he declined the program and worked part-time instead as a mechanic for one of the local automobile repair shops.

During his junior year in college, Brian worked for the college police department, where he was very popular with his peer group. The following year, the city police department hired Brian to work part-time in their internment division. After graduation, he was employed full-time as a police officer for almost six years. That satisfied his $16,000 Perkins Loan obligation. The loan was fully forgiven.

During this period, Brian not only fulfilled his student loan obligation, but he also married his college girlfriend and applied with the Federal Bureau of Investigation in Washington, D.C. He was later accepted for training at the FBI Academy and presently serves as a special agent in a large metropolitan city on the West Coast.

OTHER LOANS THAT CAN BE CANCELED

Reduction of the Stafford Loan Balance

In addition to the service-cancelable Perkins Loan, Uncle Sam has authorized the teacher service-forgiveness plan that allows the cancellation of up to $5,000 of a student's Stafford Loan, providing the loan is not in default and was initiated after October 7, 1998.

To be eligible, a borrower must work as a full-time teacher for five consecutive years in the same manner and under the same conditions required for the forgiveness of a Federal Perkins Loan; that is, teaching math, science, special education, or working in low income or teacher shortage areas. During the five-year period, the borrower is expected to repay his or her subsidized or unsubsidized loans in a normal manner. At the end of five years, the U.S. government will cancel up to $5,000 of the remaining balance of any Stafford Loan. For more detailed information, interested students should contact the school's financial aid administrator.

Loans for Health Service Professionals

There are other loans that can be erased with service. The Health Professional Student Loan, for example, assists students with exceptional need studying medicine, pharmacy, osteopathy, dentistry, optometry, or veterinary medicine. The program covers tuition plus $2,500 per year. The interest on the loan does not accrue while the student attends classes or completes a residency.

The loan may be canceled in the event of death or total disability or under the following condition: If the borrower practices in a shortage area as determined by the government, up to 85 percent of the student loan will be forgiven. The program allows for 60 percent of the loan to be forgiven during the first two years of service and another 25 percent if the participant remains for a third year in the same area. Most medical school administrators have details on the program.

Still another opportunity for professional students is the National Health Service Corps Scholarship. The program is a service-obligation scholarship designed for osteopaths seeking a master's degree, students in medical school or a physician's assistant program, or registered nurses studying to be nurse practitioners and/or certified nurse midwives.

The scholarship covers all tuition and fees plus an additional $800 per month for living expenses. The obligation is canceled upon death, permanent and total disability, or if the borrower chooses to work full-time for a period of two years at a public hospital, a rural health clinic, or a health facility with a critical shortage of nurses.

The National Health Service Corps Loan Repayment Program from the U.S. Department of Health and Human Services is available for students in certain health care fields. Eligible candidates include students who have completed at least one year of medical school or training, including medical doctors or osteopathic physicians with specialties in family medicine, general pediatrics, internal medicine, general psychiatry, or OB/GYN. Also eligible for the program are physician's assistants, nurse practitioners, nurse midwives, dentists, dental hygienists, clinical psychologists, clinical social workers, psychiatric nurse specialists, or marriage and family therapists.

The U.S. Department of Health and Human Services offers participants repayment of qualified loans if they serve for a period of two years in a medically underserved community as determined by the department. Participants are offered a competitive salary plus the repayment of $25,000 in student loans per year for two years. Candidates may request an extension of two additional years for a repayment of up to $35,000 per year thereafter, plus a stipend equal to 39 percent of the loan to compensate for additional taxes. The total value for a student who serves a qualifying community this way for four years is significant: $120,000 plus the tax stipend.[1]

Project MedSend

Finally, Project MedSend is an option for health care professionals who sense a call to full-time medical missions service. The agency offers the Student Loan Repayment Grant, designed to repay student loans owed by health-care professionals while they serve as medical missionaries in medically underserved areas of the world.

Project MedSend has six requirements for all applicants. They must (1) sense a call to use their medical training for the spread of the gospel; (2) be under the authority of a recognized Christian missions sending agency; (3) be within eighteen months of leaving for a career of medical missions service; (4) show fiscal responsibility and stewardship maturity; (5) demonstrate a missionary lifestyle; and (6) be in the process of paying off their student loans while serving their internship or residency.

Part of showing fiscal responsibility (point 4) is a student's demonstrating personal financial management that aims toward debt-free living; the medical professional should be nearly debt free except for student loans. Repayment by Project MedSend is simple: For each four-year term that a person serves on the mission field, MedSend will pay their student loan payments including interest every month. If the serving professional signs for a second four-year term, MedSend will continue to make the payments for the borrower until it is paid off or until they leave the mission field. In addition to the Student Loan Repayment Grant, Project MedSend also offers financial counseling to health-care professionals concerning student borrowing.[2]

NOTES

1. Students interested in the Health Professional Student Loan may call the National Health Service Corps at 800-638-0824. For information on the National Health Service Corp Scholarship, including an application, call 800-221-9393 or write NHSC Loan Repayment Program, 2070 Chain Bridge Road, Suite 450, Vienna, VA 22182.
2. For more information about the Student Loan Repayment Grant, call 203-891-8223 or write Project MedSend at P.O. Box 1098, Orange, CT 06470-7098; E-mail medsend@juno.com; or visit Project MedSend's website at www.medsend.org.

chapter seven

ALTERNATIVE FUNDING

As tuition and fees continue to climb, more students are opting for the cooperative education program available at over seven hundred colleges and universities throughout the United States. Thousands of students participate in a college co-op program, earning as much as $14,000 annually toward college expenses.

Perhaps the main educational attraction and advantage of cooperative programs is that classroom theory is continuously tested in the workplace. This not only results in encouraging students toward a strong work ethic, but it also helps in developing future workers who will be able to translate theory into action.

The co-op plan is also helpful in establishing roots within the business community. Many students who attend college for one quarter followed by a quarter of work (for instance, the 50/50 plan noted on the next page), find full-time employment with the same employer after graduation. Some programs allow students to attend school during the fall and spring quarters and work during the winter and summer periods.

The three types of co-op programs are:

- The AM/PM Plan—work only in the morning and attend classes every afternoon, or the opposite.
- The Day/Night Plan—work a full schedule during the day and attend classes at night.

- The 50/50 Plan—work one quarter; attend school one quarter. This plan is the most popular among students.

Most students have glowing testimonials regarding their cooperative educational experiences. "I think co-op is an excellent opportunity for students to enter the workforce. I highly recommend it to anyone who is interested in a head start," said one graduate of the program. Another co-op student attributed his present full-time job to his part-time co-op position: "I feel that participating in co-op was the best thing I did for my career. My current employer looked highly on my co-op experience and it aided me in procuring my current position."

Completion of a co-op program does not mean a job is waiting, of course. However, most employers who participate in the program have high regard for the student workers and give them fair consideration when full-time positions develop. "The students . . . have proven to be very valuable employees," explained one manager in a company using co-op students. "We have come to expect high levels of productivity from these students soon after their work term begins. The success of these students' work terms has been a major factor in the [organization's] hiring of graduates of the program for full-time positions."

Another agency using cooperative education students wrote the college's co-op director, "[Our company] has employed five different co-op students and each has made a valuable contribution. In fact, our experience with [co-op] has been so successful that we've permanently hired two of our students for very responsible positions."

For more detailed information on a specific school's co-op program, students should call or write the school's director of cooperative education.

FEDERAL PROGRAMS: SEEP AND AMERICORPS

The U.S. government also needs bright college students to keep its various agencies running smoothly. Therefore, the federal government offers the widest choice of work sites, academic opportunities, and career fields through SEEP, the Student Educational Employment Program. SEEP is open to all undergraduates as well as graduate and Ph.D. candidates. Unfortunately, most government offices know little if anything about the program. Therefore, students should contact the office for cooperative education at the college or university or call the Federal Employment Information Center in their city.

SEEP is not based on need, and students may earn up to $10,000 per year (or more, in some cases). In addition, students working in the SEEP program may receive a travel allowance as well as tuition assistance from the agency. Eligible students can work one-half day and attend classes one-half day, or alternate a quarter or semester of school with a quarter or semester of work. Normally, a cooperative education program will add one year to a student's enrollment. As Joe Re noted in *Earn & Learn*, in the mid 1990s ". . . participating students, on average, earn[ed] more than $8,500 per year toward college costs. Just think: Over the course of a four-year education, that $8,500 in annual earnings will replace $34,000 in student loans, an advantage that only multiplies after graduation. The SEEP student has valuable work experience that will likely bring him or her a higher starting salary."[1]

Another plan offered by the federal government is the Americorps program. In exchange for ten months of full-time service, Uncle Sam will provide students with an education award of $4,700 to be used for technical training or college tuition. Participants also receive housing, a uniform, a living stipend, and a weekly food allowance. Members serve in teams of ten to fifteen and live on one of five Americorps campuses in the United States. Ventures may include setting up a new 911 emergency telephone system, leading a childhood literacy program, providing living assistance to the elderly, fighting forest fires, or providing disaster relief. Skills for specific projects are taught before members begin their community efforts. Training in leadership, team building, citizenship, and physical conditioning is also provided.

Americorps is open to all young adults ages eighteen to twenty-four. For more information, contact Americorps at 800-942-2677 or on the Internet at www. americorps.org. For more information on cooperative education programs, order *Earn & Learn* from Octameron Associates, Alexandria, Virginia.[2]

SPECIALIZED COOPERATIVE PROGRAMS

Other specialized cooperative education programs may be available for qualifying students. For example, employees wanting to return to school full-time or part-time may be eligible for a company tuition plan. The employer is willing to pay for the education to improve the worker's skills, and offers the program as a company benefit. Remember, these are private funds only and should not be mistaken as unused student financial aid dollars available to all students. The fees paid by the employer are taxable; however, the expenses including tuition, books, and travel (up to $5,200) may be deducted on Schedule A, Form 1040, when filing federal income taxes. Internal Revenue Service rules change frequently, and participants in this plan should consult their company personnel office for changes.

The National Security Agency Undergraduate Training Program (NSA-UTP) offers an outstanding opportunity to students interested in studying math, computer science, computer engineering, electrical engineering, or foreign languages, and may be one of Uncle Sam's best-kept secrets. Those accepted receive four years of tuition, books, and fees at the school of their choice, a salary to cover room and board, a guarantee of employment after graduation, plus a housing allowance and travel costs to and from Fort Meade, Maryland, each summer. Student salary for the twelve-month period is $14,000 or more.

To be considered for the prestigious award, high school students must apply for NSA-UTP at the beginning of their senior year. NSA staff members carefully screen every application and only fifteen to twenty new candidates are selected annually.

Prerequisites for the NSA-UTP are similar to those required for acceptance into America's military academies. Key areas include a strong national test score and a solid high school transcript (suggested minimums include 1100 on the SAT or 25 on the ACT plus a grade point average of 3.0 or higher), outstanding references, community service, strong work ethic, and character. Beginning compensation after graduation is highly competitive with outside corporate wages.

The catch? NSA-UTP participants must maintain a 3.0 grade point average while in college and agree to work for the National Security Agency near Washington, D.C. during the summer months and for four and one-half years after graduation. Those who fail to complete their assignment are required to reimburse Uncle Sam for tuition and books.[3]

Cooperative programs can even pay for your entire education. Some colleges have their own co-op programs that provide a free college education for those willing to work on campus, including Alice Lloyd College, Pippa Passes, Kentucky; Berea College, Berea, Kentucky; and the College of the Ozarks, Point Lookout, Missouri. Contact the admissions office at each of the schools for details.[4]

NOTES

1. Joseph M. Re, *Earn & Learn,* (Alexandria, Va.: Octameron, 1995), 2.
2. Mail the request to Octameron Associates, P.O. Box 2748, Alexandria, VA 22301. Enclose $8.25 (includes shipping and handling).
3. For more information about the NSA-UTP and an application, write the National Security Agency, 9800 Savage Road, Suite 6840, Fort Meade, Maryland 20755-6840, or call 800-669-0703.
4. Phone numbers: Alice Lloyd College, 888-280-4252; Berea College, 800-326-5948; and College of the Ozarks, 417-334-6411.

chapter eight

MILITARY OPTIONS

Neither Carol nor Bill Forsyth ever thought their son, Robby, would be interested in the military. Yet, like all young boys, Robby often played with tanks and planes and made the usual grinding and crashing sounds that go along with play. But when Robby was a high school senior, he started talking about the real military; he wanted to apply at one of the military academies.

He had excellent national test scores plus an A in each of his math and science classes. Unfortunately, he found himself disqualified; too late he learned that his application needed to be submitted during his *junior* year.

Robby's older sister, Stephanie, encouraged him by mentioning another entry point to the military: the Reserve Officer Training Corps (ROTC) program. At her Christian college she received a fully paid room and board for serving as a resident assistant in her dorm, but she had heard the ROTC had a more generous financial package for students. After a few phone calls, Robby received an information packet and an application from the army ROTC. Soon after, Robby applied for a four-year ROTC scholarship and was thrilled when he passed the rigid physical and received his acceptance letter.

For Robby, it was an answer to prayer. "Wow!" he exclaimed. "A four-year scholarship, worth up to $60,000 or more, plus $1,500 every year for additional expenses."

Carol and Bill Forsyth were elated with Robby's four-year scholarship award and frequently encouraged him to strive for a cadet leadership position while in training. Robby set out to become a tank commander and earned the rank of cadet colonel while in school. Although he had missed the opportunity to apply for one of the military academies, he was happy in his new role and thrilled that he would eventually become an army officer.

THE BASIC ROTC SCHOLARSHIP

Two-, three-, and four-year ROTC scholarships are available for undergraduates at hundreds of schools across the country for a service commitment of four to eight years. The basic requirements are a good high school transcript, excellent physical condition, weight proportionate with height, and the approval of the Scholarship Acceptance Board. Students with the best chance of winning a scholarship will be in the upper 10 to 20 percent of their class, have an interest in science or engineering, score between 950 and 1100 on the SAT with 500 or more on math, communicate well on current affairs, and offer a solid reason for seeking to join the military.

The benefits for those in the program are excellent and include all tuition fees (up to $16,000 per year) plus $450 for books and a monthly stipend of $150 to help cover room and board. During the summer months, officer candidates attend six weeks of training between their sophomore and junior year and between their junior and senior year in college, all at regular service pay. Depending on the service, graduates begin their assignment as an ensign or second lieutenant.

Interested high school students must apply in the fall of their senior year. Contact the college ROTC department or write the army, navy, or air force ROTC at: Army ROTC, Gold Quest Center, P.O. Box 3279, Warminster, PA 18974; or Commander, Navy Recruiting Command/Code 314, 4015 Wilson Blvd., Arlington, VA 22203; or HQ Air Force ROTC\RROO, 551 East Maxwell Blvd., Maxwell AFB, AL 36112.

Those students already in college may also apply for two- or three-year scholarships. Additionally, students who do not qualify for a scholarship but are accepted into the advanced ROTC program will receive $150 or more per month stipend beginning in their junior year, regular service pay for the summer training camps, and a military commission as an ensign or second lieutenant.

EDUCATION BENEFITS FOR ENLISTED MILITARY PERSONNEL

Air Force Benefits

An ROTC program was the furthest thing from Barry Radcliff's mind, a college student in North Carolina. His concern was how to pay for college and the medical expenses that he and his wife were facing with the imminent arrival of their first child. Realizing his extreme financial need, Barry dropped out of college and joined the air force. Following his boot camp training, he was assigned to an aircraft maintenance department and attended college classes at night, paid for through the air force's tuition-assistance program.

Later, he was accepted into the Stripes for Bars program, which allowed him to return to college in North Carolina where he received an ROTC scholarship to cover the cost of tuition and books plus a monthly stipend. Upon graduation, Barry received a commission of second lieutenant and returned to active duty, this time as the maintenance officer over the airmen with whom he formerly worked.

Recognizing his talents and leadership skills, eighteen months later the air force sent Barry to flight training school to military transports. He pilots that aircraft to this day.

Army and Navy Medical School Training

Unfortunately, many people are either skeptical or unaware of the many military benefits available to students. Recently, a parent attending a home-school convention asked about ways to finance her daughter's medical training. She was appalled when one of the representatives suggested the army or navy medical school programs.

"The med school program would cover all of your daughter's tuition, books, lab fees, and even provide her with money for expenses in exchange for just a few years of service," he told her.

"But, what if my daughter had to go to war?" the mother asked rather indignantly.

"No problem," he answered. "If she were called into a war, she'd then be stationed in a hospital somewhere saving lives." Sadly, the woman looked down and walked away.

For more information on either medical program, interested students should contact an army or navy recruiter.

The Army Student Loan Repayment Program

Unlike the Reserve Officer Training Corps, the Army Student Loan Repayment program is for students who have already attended college and are heavily burdened with excessive student loans, whether graduated or not.

Assuming the loans are not in default, the army will pay off a maximum of $65,000 in Perkins, PLUS, and Stafford Loans for a three-year commitment as an enlisted person. If the individual has graduated from college, he or she will begin military service as a specialist E-4 and earn an additional $300 per month.

In contrast, most students employed in a nonmilitary position directly out of college would find it difficult, if not impossible, to pay off the same school loans in just three years. Even if a graduate starts out with an annual income between $30,000 and $50,000 per year, he or she would have very little for food, car payment, car insurance, rent, or entertainment after the student loan payments and all federal, state, and social security taxes were deducted. The difficulty is shown in the table below, which displays estimated tax calculations for a working single person committed to paying off $65,000 in student loans in three years. Notice, for example, that with an income of $40,000, the graduate would have only about $7,600 a year for food, auto, rent, and entertainment after paying the loan balance.

INCOME	less FIT	less SIT	less FICA	= TAKE HOME	less Loan	= Balance
$30,000	(3,460)	(1,120)	(2,295)	$23,125	(21,666)	$ 1,459
$40,000	(6,200)	(1,450)	(3,060)	$29,290	(21,666)	$ 7,624
$50,000	(7,900)	(1,900)	(3,825)	$36,375	(21,666)	$14,709

THE MONTGOMERY GI BILL

The "pro-college" Montgomery GI Bill is available for every enlisted person in the military, regardless of the branch of service. Here's how the program works: When men and women on active duty allocate $100 per month from their base salary into an educational fund for the first twelve months of service (for a total of $1,200), Uncle Sam will then add an additional amount of money to be used by the veteran for any trade school, flight school, or college in America.

The amount added can be significant. For example, for a four-year enlistment, the U.S. Marine Corps and U.S. Navy add $17,800 to the initial $1,200 in the Montgomery GI Bill, for a total of $ 19,000, plus another $11,000 in their College Fund, (a "bonus" fund offered by the services to encourage enlistment) for a total of $30,000.

The U.S. Air Force also adds $17,800 to the initial $1,200, for a total of $19,000 in benefits through the Montgomery GI Bill. In addition, active-duty men and women can earn their associates' degrees through the accredited Community College of the Air Force with the military paying up to 75 percent of all tuition costs.

Every military branch has enlistment quotas as well as enlistment tools to help their recruiting efforts. For example, in place of the College Fund, the U.S. Army can offer an incoming recruit up to $1,200 as an enlistment bonus for specific job specialties plus the Montgomery GI Bill. Interested students should phone toll-free to 800-USAArmy or check out the army's web page at www.goarmy.com.

SPECIAL NAVY PROGRAMS

When an applicant is accepted into the navy's prestigious nuclear power program, he or she will receive up to $50,000 in cash benefits for college for a six-year commitment with an opportunity to earn an associate's degree before leaving the service. In addition, the navy will pay up to 75 percent of any additional tuition costs while the person is on active duty.

To qualify, applicants must hold a certified diploma from an accredited high school, have a strong math and science background, be drug free, and pass the Navy Advanced Program Test. Opportunities exist in the missile technical field or the electronic computer area aboard submarines and the navy's newest nuclear-powered aircraft carriers.

The U.S. Navy has added another plan that may help applicants remain debt free while earning an associate's or bachelor's degree through the Navy College Assistance Student Headstart program. The plan is essentially a delayed-entry program where students attend the college of their choice for twelve months at the navy's expense (up to $18,000) prior to entering active service. Students must agree to successfully complete at least one college-level algebra class and one physics-based science course while maintaining a minimum grade point average of 2.5.

After the twelve-month period, students report to a basic training facility, then transfer to the navy's Nuclear Propulsion School where they receive two years of highly technical training, much of which is transferable to college. Those interested can go on-line at www.navyjobs.com or call 800-872-6289.

OTHER ARMY PROGRAMS FOR A COLLEGE EDUCATION

The army will help an individual wanting to earn college credits by picking up 75 percent of tuition costs through the army's ConAP (Concurrent Admissions Program). ConAP is a joint program between the army and hundreds of colleges and universities across the country. High school graduates entering the army may apply for admission into one of the participating colleges and earn college credits (later transferable to that school) while on active duty.

Assuming the candidate meets all the requirements for admission into one of the ConAP colleges, he or she will then receive a written admission guarantee from the college or university and be assigned a special college academic advisor. By participating in the plan, a student can save thousands of dollars by shortening the number of quarters or semesters needed to graduate from college.

Along with the Concurrent Admissions Program, high school graduates in critical job specialties are eligible for the army's extensive and impressive College Fund. Notice that the Army College Fund for two years' service is almost $10,000, while it can be as high as almost $31,000 for four years of service. From time to time, the other branches of the military may also offer a college fund.

THE ARMY COLLEGE SAVINGS PLAN

Time Period	Enlisted Person	GI Bill	College Fund	Total
2 years	$1,200	$15,444	$ 9,856	$26,500
3 years	$1,200	$17,808	$13,992	$33,000
4 years	$1,200	$17,808	$20,992	$40,000
4 years	$1,200	$17,808	$30,992*	$50,000

*The higher maximum payment in the College Fund is available for army personnel who serve in certain critical-shortage positions.

The tuition-assistance programs offered by the army, navy, and air force are *in addition* to the Montgomery GI Bill and the College Fund. Since many students graduating from high school are undecided about which school to attend or what courses to take, the tuition-assistance plans are exceptionally attractive for a student unsure about career objectives. Quite clearly, they also offer students an excellent way to attend college debt free.

During active duty, college credits may also be earned while enrolled in one of the Army Education Centers, through the College-Level Exam Program, through job experience, or for military courses taken while in the service.

Because all military recruiting programs are subject to change, interested students should check with a local recruiter for up-to-date details on each plan.

PROGRAMS WITH THE NATIONAL GUARD AND RESERVES

In addition to the above programs, there are other military options that provide college students with sizable earnings. For example, a student enlisted in the U.S. Army National Guard, Air National Guard, or a military reserve program can earn several hundred dollars per month while in school.

The army reserve will also pay back up to $20,000 in student loans, whether the participant is a first-year student or already graduated. The repayment is 15 percent of the student's loan for each year of service up to $10,000; for certain specialties, it increases to 15 percent of the student's loan for each year of service up to $20,000.

The reserve program can be worth up to $50,000 for a commitment of eight years (six active; two inactive). Requirements include an eight-week basic training camp plus eight weeks of advanced job training the following summer. All other training camps are two weeks in duration. Students receive up to $140 per month during the school year for attending a monthly weekend drill. (The amounts may be even higher, depending on the person's military rank.)

Additionally, once the basic and advanced training is completed, students will also receive the GI Bill benefit every month for up to thirty-six months *plus* earn another $10,000 from training camps. In some cases, students may also qualify for a $3,000 enlistment bonus.

For an eight-year commitment in the Air Force Reserve (six years active; two years inactive), the student can share in the Educational Assistance Program. Requirements include a six-week basic training camp followed by specialized job training for four to fifty-two weeks (ranging from clerk typist to air traffic controller). All other annual camps are two weeks. The Air Force Reserve will pay students up to $140 each month for attending a monthly weekend drill. Once the basic and advanced training is completed, students will also receive the GI Bill every month for up to thirty-six months. Total remuneration over the six years can be up to $31,000.

Air National Guard and National Guard participants receive the Montgomery GI Bill every month while in college (up to thirty-six months) once all training is completed. Students also receive up to $140 each month for attending a monthly weekend drill. The commitment is the same as the reserve units (six years active service; two years inactive). The Air National Guard provides twelve weeks of active-duty technical school training prior to college, which may be split between two summers, in addition to the advanced training. The Army National Guard requires eight weeks of basic training plus advanced training. Depending upon the job specialty, advanced training in both of the programs can last from four to fifty-two weeks.

The reserve and guard units offer students a monthly stipend guarantee plus competitive wages during basic and advanced training and the annual two-week summer camps.

A student loan payback is also available. Both the Air National Guard and the Army National Guard will pay back up to $10,000 in student or parent loans if the student is engaged in a specialty career field deemed critical and undermanned. Some states provide full college tuition assistance for members of the Air National Guard or Army National Guard.

While acceptance into a military academy is highly selective (about 15 percent of all applicants), the benefits, which include tuition, books, uniforms, room and board, plus a generous living allowance, are first-class for the successful candidate. America's military academies offer an outstanding education while affording students the opportunity to remain debt free.

THE U.S. MILITARY ACADEMIES

Years ago, Rick Danforth frequently upset his elementary teacher with his constant interruptions and distractions. The frustrated teacher strongly suggested that the parents put their son on a special medication to help him calm down. Instead, the parents opted to enroll Rick in a private school with smaller classes, and with the increased attention, he soon began to excel in every area.

Rick later transferred to one of the city's finest high schools where he continued to stand out, both academically and spiritually. During this time, Rick's father contacted his U.S. senator in Washington, D.C., and requested information regarding an appointment to a military academy for his son. After careful scrutiny of Rick's academic records and extensive interviews with the senator's staff members, Rick received an appointment to the U.S. Air Force Academy, where he was accepted and became a star cadet, helping others with their flight training. Since the government paid for his education, the family was able to save money for his younger sister to attend college while Rick earned his wings and flew F-16s for the U.S. Air Force.

The basic admissions requirements to the U.S. military academies include minimum scores of 1100 to 1300 on the SAT with a minimum of 600 on math (a recent West Point class averaged 650 on math and 630 on the verbal). The academies also expect the applicants to be in the top 20 percent of their class (in some cases, 10 percent), and well rounded in athletics, school, civic, and church activities. All academies except the U.S. Coast Guard require a congressional appointment. (A U.S. congressman or senator must nominate the student.) The normal commitment following graduation is five or more years as an active-duty officer. For academy addresses and phone numbers, see the next page.

The military is not for everyone; however, students who select one of the military options have the opportunity to graduate from college without being entrapped with thousands of dollars in student loans. Whether it's receiving a free education at one of the academies or through the ROTC program, students who perform military service will enjoy a largely debt-free college education.

APPLYING TO THE U.S. MILITARY ACADEMIES

Interested high school students should apply at one of the following academies during the spring of their junior year, submitting the congressional nomination with the application. (The student should contact the Washington, D.C., office of one of the two senators or the local state congressman to start the process.)

The Air Force Academy

U.S. Air Force Academy
2304 Cadet Drive Admissions
Colorado Springs, CO 80840-5025
800-443-9266
Web site: www.usafa.af.mil

Annapolis

U.S. Naval Academy
117 Decatur Road
Annapolis, MD 21402-5018
800-638-9156
Web site: www.nadn.navy.mil

The Coast Guard

U.S. Coast Guard Academy
15 Mohegan Avenue
New London, CT 06320-4195
860-444-8500
Web site: www.uscg.mil

USMM Academy

U.S. Merchant Marine Academy
Kings Point, NY 11024-1699
800-732-6267
Web site: www.usmma.edu

West Point

U.S. Military Academy
606 Thayer Road
West Point, NY 10996-1797
800-822-8762
Web site: www.usma.edu

chapter nine

MONEY MANAGEMENT FOR STUDENTS

Y ou watch. One of these days, my ship is going to come in," Charles Denning told his friends year after year. Charlie, as most of his friends called him, didn't think college was important, although he had attended the local community college for two quarters. "It's just not for me. Besides, I can make plenty of money working where I want to work, and I get to drive a different car every day," he boasted.

"He's good, and he's got this idea that he's really going to make it big. I like that in my salespeople," said Charlie's manager at the automobile dealership where he was a used-car salesman. Charlie was the dealership's top producer every month, and he purchased multiple lottery tickets each payday. Almost everyone liked Charlie's positive attitude, including a young girl named Suzanne whom he met at the dealership. Soon after they met, they were married, and she was often heard telling the same tale, "Someday Charlie's ship will come in."

Then it happened. Suddenly Charlie had more friends than he ever dreamed possible. Hundreds of people called and dropped by Charlie and Suzanne's apartment to congratulate him. Charlie had won the lottery. In fact, the fat $20 million purse was "his ship."

One of the most amazing transformations took place, at least in Charlie's mind. Without any formal management training, Charlie determined that he was instantly bright enough to purchase and run his own automobile dealership, which he proudly called Denning Automotive Sales.

As a betting man, he liked to play the horses—and he decided to own some. Shortly after his "ship" arrived, Charlie was deeply involved in racehorses, two automobile dealerships, and a divorce. Determined to live out his dream, Charlie found another girlfriend and was married for the second time. He then began to travel from city to city, always watching and hoping that one of his horses would bring him additional fame and fortune. To relax, Charlie contacted a Florida boat dealership and purchased a high-speed powerboat, often called a "Cigar Boat" because of its long pointed nose.

Back at home, there was a slowdown on new-car sales, and soon one of Charlie's automobile dealerships began to fail. To add to his financial troubles, none of Charlie's horses ever provided a positive cash flow as part of his overall money-making scheme. "I'd get more money selling them to a glue manufacturer," he grumbled one day.

As the financial pressure began to mount and his ship began to sink, Charlie started borrowing money in hopes of keeping everything afloat. Unfortunately, his $20 million didn't last long; neither did his second marriage. Eventually, Charlie filed for bankruptcy in the U.S. Bankruptcy Court. While his ship had provided instant wealth, it did not provide instant wisdom, leadership, or money management skills. Instead, it left Charlie with two broken marriages, two failed auto dealerships, and over $5 million in debt.

"It's not how much money you have, but how you manage what you do have," said founder and president of Christian Financial Concepts, Larry Burkett, to a caller on his national radio talk show.

One student graduated with an MBA in business, yet never learned the basics of money management. As a result, the graduate soon became bogged down with car payments, house payments, furniture payments, student loan payments, insurance payments, department store payments, and high credit card payments. Since the young man did not have a spending plan, he ended up completely entrapped in financial bondage for years.

THE BASICS OF MONEY MANAGEMENT

No matter how little or how much your family has, money management is essential. That truth applies not only to parents but to their grown children during the college years, whether living at school or commuting from home. In order to survive financially, college students need to understand how to manage their money at school.

During the last decade, the role of paying for college shifted from the parents to the student. As a result, more students are opting for student loans than ever before. Today, over 60 percent of all financial aid is government-backed student or parent loans, and as costs continue to rise, student borrowing continues to escalate as well.

"Student loans are not the problem. The problem is students who borrow in excess of what they need to get a college education," Burkett has said.

A Wise Spending Plan

For those students who desire to graduate with the least amount of debt, it is critical that they maintain complete control of their spending while in school. One of the best ways is to have a flexible and well-thought-out spending plan. Basically, a spending plan, or budget, is nothing more than a financial guide to help students meet their needs without going into debt. Like a road map, a spending plan can help direct students where they are going as well as where they have been. When future college costs are compared to future financial aid, the need for money management becomes even more apparent.

I recommend the following formula to control spending in school (and upon graduation as well):

TAF MINUS T&T = NAF

This spending formula may seem complex, but once we define terms it should be clear. The plan is easy to use and highly versatile. More importantly, the plan will help track and develop proper spending habits prior to graduation.

Here are some definitions. TAF is *total available funds*. This embraces all incoming finances from all sources regardless of the amount, including money from parents, aunts, uncles, savings accounts, college loans, student employment, grants, and scholarships.

T&T is *taxes and tithe*. Although most students do not have to pay taxes while in school, taxes will play an important role in the management of the student's income following graduation. The second *T* is for tithe as students offer a portion of their earnings to their place of worship.

NAF is *net available funds*. Once students have noted all incoming finances and deducted applicable taxes and tithe, the remaining amount, known as net available funds, is the money available for housing, food, books, tuition, travel, and every other conceivable expense known to college students worldwide.

To properly execute a spending plan, students must list the items to be purchased with the remaining funds. Some of the expenditures will fall under a category known as "fixed" expenses, or those items that remain virtually the same each month. Examples may include rent, tuition, car payments, and car insurance.

On the other hand, "variable" expenses such as food, clothing, entertainment, utilities, or money for unexpected repairs or gifts are extremely difficult to budget or plan for.

The sample college-spending plan found in appendix 12 has suggested categories and accompanying worksheets for students to use as a guide. The figures to be posted in each category are the students' own numbers, and the allocation of the funds should be given serious consideration. For instance, if a student allocated three-fourths of all available funds for food (easy to do if the student plans to eat out often), very little would be left for books, clothes, oil changes, etc.

In order for the plan to work effectively, the figures must be flexible. For example, students may allocate money into one area and later find it is more than necessary. At that point, some of the dollars can then be moved to another category that may be running short. By keeping the spending plan up-to-date and flexible, every student will know at a glance how much money is available and avoid the dangerous temptation of overspending and going into debt.

Upon Graduation

After graduation, many students are tempted to buy some of the necessities they were deprived of while in school. *Now I have an income; I'll be able to pay this off,* Cheri thinks. *I'm ready for a new sofa that's not stained or a battered hand-me-down.* The thought seems to make sense, but often it leads to excesses, such as a washer and dryer, even though there's a nearby Laundromat and Cheri washes only two loads a week. And while the latest megawatt home theater system (which some of her friends have) would be enjoyable, Cheri would be ignoring a basic purchasing principle: Graduates should rely on their spending plan to determine ways to purchase the items *with cash.* That's much safer than signing on the dotted line for twelve, twenty-four, or thirty-six months, more than likely at very high interest rates.

A proper spending plan will not allow for deficit spending as habitually exercised by the federal government. By seeking wise counsel, tracking expenses, eliminating impulsive buying, and avoiding high interest loans, everyone can avoid financial bondage, whether they are single professionals, married couples, or students seeking to graduate debt free.

USING CREDIT CARDS

One way students can help themselves remain free of financial bondage is by avoiding the credit card trap. Technically speaking, the credit card is an incredible advancement in the world of finances. The ease and simplicity of the system is amazing. If a person carries a major credit card such as a VISA, MasterCard, or American Express, there is little need for currency, whether in a restaurant in Iowa City, Maui, or Bangkok.

In her book, *The Ultimate Credit Handbook,* author and speaker, Gerri Detweiler, says, "A credit card is nothing more than a means of accessing a personal loan, but because of the glitzy advertising, few people think of a card that way. Instead we think of credit cards as a means of convenience, a shortcut to the 'good life,' symbols of financial success, or even an extension of our income."[1]

I know one college student who began collecting credit cards as a status symbol. By his twentieth birthday, he had amassed some eighteen gasoline and department store cards, five VISA Gold cards, five MasterCards, one American Express card, and over $10,000 of debt. As the pressure for payment increased, he began to borrow funds from one card in order to pay the minimum on another. He had become a slave to the lenders; he was caught in the trap.

Are the banks that offer the credit cards to blame for anyone getting caught in the trap? The answer is no, not directly. The cards are not the problem. It's the misuse of the card that plagues everyone, including many college students.

Most banks portray an image of solidarity with their customers and promote their "interest-free grace period." The truth is, if a student opts to pay just the minimum, there is no grace period. Once a minimum payment is sent to a bank, the grace period is canceled. From that point on, the remaining balance is subject to the maximum prevailing rate; that interest is charged and begins to accrue immediately on every purchase until the balance is paid in full. As a result, once caught in the trap, it's almost impossible to escape.

Pay the Minimum Amount?

When addressing students on the subject of credit, Detweiler references the minimum-payment syndrome as a very clever means contrived by the banks to make lots of money. As an example of how this works, she explains, "If a [student] has a balance of $1,000 on a credit card with an annual fee of $20 at a interest rate of nearly 20 percent, and chooses to pay only the minimum of 3 percent of the unpaid balance each month, it will take eight years to pay the debt, cost $843 in finance charges and $108 in membership fees for a total of $2, 023."[2]

Look again: The $1,000 has ballooned to $2,023—a doubling of the amount due and taking eight years to repay. However, those who do budget for each purchase and make the full payment every month in order to avoid finance charges must watch out for a different problem Some banks charge their credit card customers a $25.00 service charge if the cardholder continually pays the full amount due. Avoid those banks that penalize you for immediately paying off your balance.

College students are big targets for the lending institutions. "Credit card issuers routinely bombard students with offers, by E-mail, by stuffing them in bookstore bags, and by giving them away with a free T-shirt," wrote Margaret Mannix in *U.S. News & World Report*.[3] In their zeal to capture the college market, credit card companies spend millions of dollars each year promoting their cards on campus. You may want credit, but they want your interest payments—and they often charge high rates thinking that with little or no past credit, you will pay for it. In many cases, the bank's only requirement is a student ID card. "College students have it easy when it comes to getting credit cards. They don't need an income or even a parent's signature to get a card," said Detweiler. "All they do is sign on the dotted line and the plastic is in the mail." Obtaining credit cards during college is easy, Detweiler concluded, because "the big banks woo the college students . . . knowing that most cardholders keep their cards well after graduation."[4]

Robert Bugai, president of New Jersey-based College Marketing Intelligence, noted that some students fill out credit card applications as soon as they arrive on campus. "The financial services industry probably outspends all others when it come to campus promotions."[5]

Yes, the opportunities to get "free money," also known as credit card debt, abound at many colleges. Even the campus bookstores often get in the act. Bookstores will often have a table set up with credit card applications along with a choice of free gifts. "The free gifts are used as a hook to get students to apply," said Bugai. "The problem is that students can apply ten times and each time receive another free gift."

The credit card companies also promote the available cash with the cards. "Instead of merchandise, take the money." Most banks are eager to have students use their cards for cash withdrawals. Students often forget (or don't read the fine print) that at the moment of withdrawal, the bank collects a set fee, usually 2 percent, as a service charge. That's in addition to the usual high interest rate on the balance it creates on your credit card account from that day forward.

With so much credit available to students, it comes as no surprise that many are in financial trouble before graduation. If a student goes on a credit card binge and is unable to make the required payments, he or she will not only end up with poor credit, but may also have problems getting a job, attending graduate school, or even renting an apartment. Bugai also notes that it's not uncommon for students to declare bankruptcy.

Recently I heard a radio broadcast in which a woman caller described the tragic consequences of opening so many credit card accounts. She and her husband found themselves deep in debt after college graduation, placing the blame on the ease of acquiring credit cards. "My husband and I ended up with a total of fourteen credit cards we received while we were college students," the twenty-five-year-old woman told the radio host. "Then after we got married and had two children, our medical bills started adding up until we finally had to file personal bankruptcy." Referring to all the gifts students receive when they sign up for a new credit card, she added, "The free T-shirt is not worth it."

WISE USE OF A CREDIT CARD

Debt comes in various shapes and styles and is often preceded by pleasure. Using a credit card for gasoline, clothes, and nice restaurants is not wrong. It is only the misuse of credit cards that will eventually come back to haunt students.

How can students use credit cards wisely, so the card is an ally rather than a threat? Most financial advisors agree on the following guidelines:

1. Open only one credit card account while in college.
2. Use the card sparingly and only when funds are available to pay the total invoice amount when it's due.
3. If a major emergency arises and cash is not immediately available (for instance, a mechanical breakdown of the car) use the card, but begin to pay back as much as you can every month. Do not pay just the minimum amount but the maximum to avoid piling up the finance charges. If possible, ask a family member to help pay off some or all of the credit bill, and then repay the member quickly; your parents or other family members probably will not charge interest.
4. Shop for a credit card with no annual fee, a twenty-five day grace period, and a low interest rate. Banks are required to reveal their interest rates up front, so this information is available. Unfortunately, the banks are permitted by law to change their interest rates with only a two-week written notice to cardholders.
5. Report any lost or stolen card to the bank within forty-eight hours; that will limit liability to only $50 in unauthorized charges. If the loss is not discovered and reported to the bank within the designated time, a student can be held liable for up to $500 in fraudulent charges.

Our society breeds on credit and credit cards, and as a result, consumer credit accounts are available to everyone. One graduate found the ease of acquiring credit cards led directly to excessive spending and thousands of dollars of debt.

Eventually she turned to a nationally recognized nonprofit organization called Consumer Credit Counseling Service that worked out a plan to repay all her creditors and restore her credit rating. This agency can be very helpful in setting a strategy and winning both support and relief from creditors who want *all* your money *now* and have put on the pressure. For more information and the nearest location, students may call 800-388-2227.

STRATEGIES FOR MAJOR PURCHASES

There is another "trap" awaiting the unsuspecting student. Occasionally, a group of roommates will collectively pick out new furniture for their college apartment. Whether you're in college or a college graduate sharing a place, that's a good idea; however, don't rent the furniture. The rent-to-own stores represent a trap for most young adults. Many college and singles' apartments receive very harsh treatment, and what seems like a minor decision can produce major headaches and horrendous user fees, often higher than the cost of the furniture if purchased at a major retail store. In addition, new furniture rented monthly for several years will almost always cost more than a direct purchase. Instead, college students should shop at neighborhood garage sales and used furniture outlets. The Salvation Army and Goodwill Industries often have good used furniture at reasonable prices, and you can feel good knowing your dollars are helping worthwhile charitable organizations.

One fundamental purchase every student will face someday is budgeting for a car, either one's first or a replacement. Because most new automobiles lose up to 35 percent of their value in the first year, it makes good economic sense to shop for a quality used car or end-of-lease vehicle.

Except in business situations, or for the person who can afford a new automobile every two years, automobile leasing is not recommended. The leasing of products has been around for many decades, but it was not until the 1980s that auto leasing took on a new dimension. Saddled with massive inventories, the automobile manufacturers found that consumers would respond in great numbers when offered a manufacturer's rebate or special leasing incentive. In many cases, consumers end up paying more when leasing an automobile. At the end of the term, they have nothing to show for it. The car is not theirs, and they may have to pay an "excessive use" charge if the mileage exceeds the allowable limits on the lease contract. Nevertheless, this method of doing business has carried forward to this day and promises to be a major player in all areas of business during the twenty-first century.

YOUR CHECKING ACCOUNT

Having a checking account makes a lot of sense. It lets you pay recurring bills by mail and ends the need to carry a lot of cash around. A well-kept checking account can qualify you for one quality credit card account with reasonable terms. But there are some cautions.

Keeping Account Transactions Current

Some students end up paying exorbitant bank fees while in college. Why? Because their checks "bounce." They don't maintain sufficient funds in the account to cover their checks. The problem is they fail to perform basic record keeping.

Remember, you should enter each check the same day (even hour) it is signed. Then subtract the check amount from the balance, creating a new, up-to-date balance. Better yet, order duplicate checks from the bank so you will always have a copy of every check written and avoid the possibility of forgetting to post an entry.

Once the account is opened, the bank will send regular statements itemizing all the transactions that have occurred in the previous month. We'll discuss how to balance a checkbook shortly. The following tips may help students avoid "insufficient funds" charges. First, keep an accurate record of every check, and enter it in the check register quickly. Second, save all ATM and debit card receipts and subtract each amount from the checkbook balance on a daily basis.

To cover costs, most banks add a monthly service charge. Since the charges vary from bank to bank, a thrifty student will shop around for the best plan. Of course, these charges also need to be added into the checkbook register in order to maintain a proper balance.

Balancing the Checkbook

Balancing a checking account once a month is simply a matter of perseverance and patience. Ultimately, a student's checkbook will balance with the monthly bank statement and provide an ample historical record of most major expenditures.

The following five steps for balancing a checking account will help students avoid 90 percent of all costly bank charges. First, the student should note which checks have been paid by the bank by placing a mark in the checkbook register next to each check shown on the statement from the bank. Second, the student should compare all ATM (automatic teller machines) and check card receipts with the bank statement. Students should follow the same procedure as in the first step, marking off each debit in both the checkbook register and the statement.

Next, if the statement does not show outstanding checks already written or recent ATM and check card transactions, students should list each on the back of the statement page and total the column. Step four is just like the previous step, except it lists all deposits not shown on the statement. If the statement does not indicate recent deposits, these also need to be noted on the back of the statement page and totaled.

The final step is simply to perform the required calculations. Adding every deposit not shown on the statement to the statement balance and deducting all checks not revealed will provide the *true balance*. If that figure matches with the student's checkbook register, the account is in balance and needs no additional attention. Students unable to balance are encouraged to ask the trained professionals at their local bank branch for assistance.

Using a Debit Card with the Account

Some students carry a debit check card with a VISA or MasterCard logo. While it looks and acts much like a credit card and can be used for credit card purchases as well, this two-in-one card when used for a check card purchase immediately debits a student's checking account. The downside is this: A check card is basically an electronic check and anyone can use it wherever a credit card is accepted. Since the money is deducted directly from the bank, a thief is able to clear out a student's entire checking account in a matter of minutes. Because of that, students should use a debit card cautiously and only on a limited basis.

If a check card is lost or stolen, the risk to the student is the same as a credit card. If the bank is notified within the allotted forty-eight hours, the bank will only hold the student responsible for up to $50 in charges. However, students need to be aware that if the bank is not notified within forty-eight hours, the bank can hold the student responsible for up to $500 in unauthorized charges.

NOTES

1. Gerri Detweiler, *The Ultimate Credit Handbook* (New York: Penguin, 1993), 55.
2. Ibid., 66.
3. Margaret Mannix, U.S. News Online at www.usnews.com/usnews/edu/student/stcred.html, "Credit Card Binge," February 2000.
4. Detweiler, *The Ultimate Credit Handbook*, 116.
5. Robert Bugai, "Easy Credit Yields Hard Lessons for College Students," *Money Matters* (April 1996), 6.

chapter ten

STRATEGIES FOR PAYING FOR COLLEGE

As noted earlier, paying for college can be one of the most challenging times parents and students ever face. While a $25,000 automobile can be amortized over a period of three to six years, in most cases, student tuition fees and room and board—projected at almost $16,000 in 2001 and climbing every year—must be paid in advance.

The key responsibility for budgeting begins ahead of enrollment, with the student's parents. Some colleges have enlisted the help of outside organizations to spread the tuition payments over a period of twelve months. Generally, the outside provider makes the heavy tuition payments to the school at the beginning of each quarter or semester, while receiving monthly payments from the parents and students. In many cases the plans are interest free, though they require a small annual fee.

To learn about the procedure and whether the school you're considering participates, contact the financial aid administrator at the college or university or call any of these service providers: Knight College Resource Group, 800-225-6783; Tuition Management Systems, 800-722-4867; Academic Management Service, 800-635-0120; Facts Management System, 800-624-7092; or USA Group, 800-348-4605.

Some schools have put into place a tuition guarantee plan that guarantees costs will not increase for two, three or even four years. Some require a deposit, others a prepayment. For instance, Howard Payne University in Brownwood, Texas, guarantees the same tuition costs for all four years provided the student remains continuously enrolled (except for summer breaks) and completes twelve credit units per semester.

Some schools will consider a tuition reduction for children of alumni. Others offer a reduced fee for returning adults, when two or more family members are enrolled simultaneously, or when the college actively employs the student.

WHEN TO START SAVING

Colleges are helping to contain the tuition explosion with such programs as monthly payments, a tuition lock, and tuition reduction for children of alumni or several students from the same family. Still, the best way to be able to afford the high cost of higher education is to have significant savings whenever possible. And it is possible to develop strategies for saving—and to begin saving now, when children are young.

As college costs continue to leap forward, the need grows for parents with young children to commit to a savings program for their children's education. If you have a three-year-old daughter in 2000, and she enters college in 2015, she would face a projected four-year bill for tuition, room and board, books, and living expenses of $117,000! That's for a state college education; the cost for a four-year education at a private college would be double that, or $240,000. (See appendix 13 for projected college costs and necessary savings for other years.)

Ideally, students and parents should have a savings/investment account to pay for college without going into debt. However, many don't, tempted by the promise of so-called "cheap" loan money. David Cincotta, the founder and president of CollegeNOW, a national prepaid tuition plan, has described the problem well. "With so much 'cheap' money available in government-backed student loans and with college costs rising at double the consumer inflation rate, families have stopped saving for college. The answer to America's need to educate our children is not more debt, but savings."[1]

WHERE TO START SAVING

Once parents decide they want to begin a savings program for their children, the question is where—what kind of savings account in what kind of financial institution? In the past, saving institutions remained the method of choice for most family savings, often sheltered in statement savings accounts. The money was secure and guaranteed by the FDIC (Federal Deposit Insurance Corporation). The most obvious advantage was accessibility. People could withdraw their money at any time, without a penalty, from thousands of ATM locations around the world. In addition, the institutions paid the owner a small fee, or interest, for storing their money in the bank, typically less than the rate of inflation.

That low rate of return, of course, remains the drawback of having such funds readily available. However, if the funds are not needed for seven, ten, or even fifteen years for a college education, parents can obtain much larger returns by placing the money in different kinds of savings and investment accounts. Such accounts offer higher returns that not only beat inflation but enjoy the benefits of compounding (shown in the table "Big Gains with Small Investments" on page 107). In fact, during the last decade, many people began to place their savings into other types of interest-bearing accounts, Roth IRAs and the new educational IRAs, as well as the more traditional money-market accounts and certificates of deposit (CDs).

CDs and Money Market Accounts

Many regard CDs as the safest type of investment, because they are guaranteed by the FDIC against loss by the financial institution. In addition, the interest rates on bank CDs are three to four percentage points higher than statement savings; the longer the term, generally the higher the interest, which is locked for the entire term of the certificate. However, there are costly penalties for those who suddenly have a financial need and want to withdraw their funds. Thus the parents must be committed to leaving the funds untouched, devoted only to savings for college. While both statement savings and certificates of deposit are safe and offer little risk, both are tied to the inflation index, which can result in a loss of buying power.

A more flexible method is the money market account available from banks and stock firms. Money market funds are safe, generate slightly higher interest than savings accounts, and can be redeemed at any time without incurring a penalty. They also provide an excellent short-term method for those who want to have immediate access while earning a more lucrative interest rate.

Educational and Roth IRAs

The reauthorization of the Higher Education Act in 1997 introduced the educational IRA. Families earning less than $160,000 are entitled to deposit up to $500 per year, per child, into an Education IRA. The earnings are tax-free when used for college tuition, fees, books, and room and board. The major drawback is the $500 limit imposed on each family. Even with the power of compounding, the parents probably will need to save more than $500 a year (even if started at the child's birth) to pay for a child's college education. The IRA can be rolled over to another member of the family; however, if the funds are not used for higher education, they are taxable and subject to a 10 percent penalty. The Education IRA can make a good investment for parents with limited funds for saving but still desiring to develop a college fund for their young children. The other disadvantage is that the IRA cannot be used in conjunction with the Hope Scholarship and the Lifetime Learning Credit. Thus it offers limited opportunities for the average family. For more details, see appendix 8.

As a college savings program, the benefits from a Roth IRA are somewhat limited as well. Depending on income, each parent may be eligible to put up to $2,000 into a Roth IRA every year. The higher-deposit level of the Education IRA will mean more funds accumulating tax-free for a college education. There also is flexibility. Not all funds from the Roth IRA must be used for education; some or all can be left for retirement or other needs, although a penalty will occur if withdrawn early. However, there is no penalty for early withdrawal when used for educational expenses. The key advantage, of course, is that you don't have to pay taxes on the growth. The key disadvantage is that the deposits are taxable; parents have to pay the taxes ahead of time when they are in a higher tax bracket. And as the parents' income increases, the amount allowed for investment decreases (see appendix 8 for details).

A Custodial Account

Another way to save money for your child is to open a custodial account. The Uniform Gift to Minors Account (UGMA) custodial program allows parents to select when, where, and how their children's savings are to be invested. With this plan, a custodian is selected, typically the parent, and that custodian makes the investment decisions for the child as to where the money will be placed. When money leaves the account, it must be spent solely for the benefit of the child. Prior to age eighteen or twenty-one, depending on the state, the custodian determines the child's spending decisions.

The tax benefits of the UGMA are substantial. For example, as the account grows, the actual earnings on the account are taxed at the child's lower tax rate. If the child is less than fourteen years of age, the first $750 of investment income earned by the child each year, i.e., interest, dividends, and capital gains, is totally tax-free. The next $750 of unearned income is taxed at the child's rate, as are all unearned funds for those ages fourteen or older. All unearned income over the initial $1,500 is then taxed at the parent's marginal tax rate. For additional information and updates, parents should contact their financial or tax advisor.

Another advantage of the UGMA account is that the custodian may use the funds to purchase investments, e.g., stocks, bonds, and/or mutual funds. The huge disadvantage is that neither the donor nor the custodian can place any conditions on the funds once the minor becomes an adult, usually eighteen in most states. As an adult, he or she may choose to spend the UGMA funds for something other than a college education.

THE POWER OF COMPOUNDING

Whatever the type of savings account parents begin for their children, the principle is always the same: Save earlier and often. Systematic (usually monthly) saving, begun in the children's younger years, is the best approach. Leaving the interest with the principal year after year will result in major growth of the child's college funds. The time value of money and the principle of compounding are powerful concepts. If implemented over the first twenty years of a child's life, this method offers an excellent opportunity to pay for college.

"Compounding is mankind's greatest invention because it allows for the reliable, systematic accumulation of wealth," Albert Einstein once acknowledged. It only takes a small amount of money to reach an astonishing gain when the savings are coupled with the power of compounding.

For instance, suppose as a parent you began investing $50 a month when the child is seven. By the time he is eighteen, the $600 a year you invested would total $6,600, but by reinvesting all interest, the figure is $11,943 based on a 10 percent return. The table below illustrates the dynamic effect of interest compounding with sample investment returns of 5 and 10 percent. Notice that a child whose parents have invested since his birth through age twenty will have tripled his investment amount.

BIG GAINS WITH SMALL INVESTMENTS[2]

Years	Amount Invested	5% Return	10% Return
1	$ 600	$ 614	$ 628
2	1,200	1,259	1,322
3	1,800	1,938	2,089
4	2,400	2,651	2,936
5	3,000	3,400	3,872
6	3,600	4,188	4,906
7	4,200	5,016	6,048

Years	Amount Invested	5% Return	10% Return
8	$ 4,800	$ 5,887	$ 7,309
9	5,400	6,802	8,703
10	6,000	7,764	10,242
11	6,600	8,775	11,943
12	7,200	9,838	13,822
13	7,800	10,955	15,898
14	8,400	12,130	18,190
15	9,000	13,364	20,724
16	9,600	14,662	23,522
17	10,200	16,026	26,613
18	10,800	17,460	30,028
19	11,400	18,967	33,801
20	12,000	20,552	37,968

ABOUT MUTUAL FUNDS INVESTING

Many families today are investing in no-load mutual funds; mutual funds are typically investment funds composed of a collection of stocks or bonds (or a combination of the two) that have historical rates of return much higher than CDs or money market funds. The risk can be low, moderate, or high, depending on the particular fund, and yet, over a long period of investing for college (five years or more), those risks are diminished.

The approach among those investing for college has been aggressive-growth funds for younger parents, more conservative funds for parents with teens. Mutual funds allow investors to pool their resources with thousands of other investors to buy stock in numerous companies. Each fund has a fund manager who continually moves investors' money to provide the greatest return.

While the risk is higher than institutional savings, it is not as high as purchasing individual bonds or corporate stocks because the money is spread over a wide range of companies. Depending on the investment firm's policy, investors normally have immediate access to their money.

By investing in companies in the Dow Jones Industrial Average (DJIA) or similar companies, earnings may increase at a sizable rate of return as evidenced by comparing a standard savings fund to Wall Street investments during a sixteen-year historical period. The chart on the next page shows the superior returns typical of a mutual fund patterned after the DJIA. Rates of return for mutual funds do fluctuate, of course; there are years when a CD actually outperformed mutual funds, when mutual funds had minimal or even negative returns. The investor must be willing to let the fund remain several years, to ride out year-to-year volatility. Parents of future college students usually have that long time frame required.

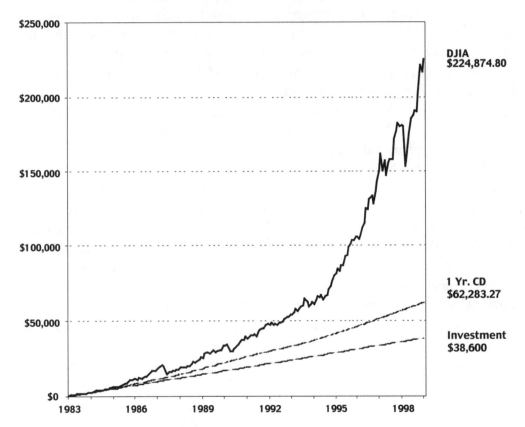

**Comparison of Returns of the DJIA
Versus an Average Bank CD
During the Sixteen Years Ending 1999**

The above returns are based on consecutive monthly investments of $200 beginning July 1, 1983 and continuing until June 30, 1999. During that period, the DJIA compound total rate of return was 18.3 percent per year versus the compound rate of 6.6 percent for an average bank CD. These are historical rates and future performance may differ. Illustration is for planning assistance only and is not intended to project the performance of any specific or real investment product.

ABOUT STATE TUITION PLANS

Two Types of Programs

According to David Cincotta, the fastest-growing programs in America to help parents with high college tuition costs are the so-called 529 (named after Section 529 of the IRS Code) or Qualified State Tuition Plans (STP). Most state programs allow parents to pay into them, either in one lump sum annually or on a monthly basis. If your state offers such a program, it's well worth considering. Here's how it works. There are two types of programs: (1) state prepaid tuition plans that guarantee the plan will cover future tuition costs at all state colleges and universities, and (2) the state college savings plans that do not give the same guarantee but offer a potentially higher rate of return. Your state's STP will be one of these two. The rate of return is not guaranteed and the family assumes the investment risk.

Both programs allow the student to use the proceeds for tuition and other educational expenses such as room and board. However, a significant drawback exists for most state prepaid tuition programs: The student loses the tuition guarantee if he or she selects a private college or an out-of-state school.

While neither plan guarantees admission, they do allow the family to defer federal taxation on the growth of their investment until the student matriculates. The student then pays federal income tax at his or her lower tax rate on the increased value of the education received. All state programs grant state tax exemption to their residents, and some even allow a deduction for the prepaid amounts.

Money magazine columnist, Lani Luciano, wrote, "You prepay tuition for the number of years or courses you desire either in a lump sum or in monthly installments. When college rolls around, the value of credits in your state college system is all paid up. Whether a prepaid plan turns out to be a wise investment will depend on how quickly tuition rises in your state and whether and where your kid attends college."[3]

Refund Policies

The most frequently asked question is, "What about a refund should a student decide not to attend college, or elect to attend a college in another state, or move out of state prior to the fulfillment of the plan?"

Some of the programs are more liberal in their refund policy than others. For example, Ohio's prepaid tuition plan provides full coverage at all tuition cost when Mom and Dad put $15,900 into Ohio's prepaid tuition plan for a newborn.[4] By the time the child is ready to attend college, most or all of the tuition costs will be covered at any of the state's thirteen public post secondary schools. Of course, many parents do not have $16,000 available for a lump sum investment; the option then is to pay smaller amounts annually or monthly, but such payments must increase each year to reflect tuition gains. "What if your kid decides to motorcycle around the world at age seventeen instead of ever hitting the books?" noted Luciano, "Then, you get a refund." (A refund in Ohio's plan is 100 percent of accrued funds less a 10 percent federal tax penalty on earnings.)

Keep in mind that programs vary from state to state in their refund policy as well as their initial investment procedure. Some states only return the original investment while others refund the principal plus interest. For instance, Tennessee offers no refund before the student reaches the age of eighteen; after that, the refund equals the principal plus 50 percent of the increase.

Reporting on the Internet (www.finaid.org), Mark Kantrowitz listed two types of plans for contributing to a state's STP: (1) *the prepaid unit,* in which the parent buys shares that represent a fixed percentage of a year's tuition (everyone pays the same for the shares with the price of the shares increasing yearly); and (2) *contracts,* which require that the parents agree to purchase a specified number of years of tuition. The purchase price depends on whether the payment is on a lump sum or installment *and* the age of the child.

The CollegeNow Tuition Plan

A new type of prepaid program is the CollegeNOW National Prepaid Tuition Plan that will guarantee prepaid tuition at hundreds of private and state schools across the country. The plan allows families to purchase college education at thousands of schools nationwide at a discount from the present prevailing tuition. The prepaid tuition can then be redeemed at any college or university participating in the CollegeNOW program. For information on CollegeNOW Company LLC, log on to www.collegenow.com or call 877-9-COLLEGE. For additional information on the state prepaid tuition and savings plans, contact the state office as noted in appendix 14.

CollegeNOW president David Cincotta gives the following advice before purchasing any prepaid plan: (1) Make sure the plan offers an unqualified guarantee in writing that the student will receive a college education in the future regardless of the price of tuition; and (2) verify the plan will "keep pace with the rate of inflation at all participating schools, not just the 'average' college.

"The best prepaid plans will also offer the student the opportunity to choose from all types of institutions nationally including state and private schools, liberal arts colleges, technical schools, and Christian colleges," Cincotta notes, "as well as the option for in-state and out-of-state tuition. In addition, the ideal plan will be tax-exempt so that neither the parent nor the student will be taxed at the federal or state level on the increased value of the prepaid education. And finally, parents should be allowed to pay for the prepaid tuition plan at their convenience including a single lump-sum payment, monthly payments or even quarterly payments."[5]

Noting that by 2002 student borrowing may had reached almost $52 billion, Cincotta warns, "We may soon see college graduates who owe $100,000 or more in student debt. The answer to America's need to educate our children is not more debt, but savings!" CollegeNOW will help make savings a reality for thousands of families," Cincotta added.

NOTES

1. David Cincotta, "Prepaid Plans," contained in personal correspondence to the author, 12 December 1999.
2. This assumes the rate of return is compounded monthly. For other examples of compounding, contact DeBoer and Associates, CPAs, 12165 West Center Road, Suite 72, Omaha, Nebraska 68144, or phone 402-333-5200.
3. Lani Luciano, "Consider a Prepaid Tuition Plan," Money, March 1997, 37.
4. This figure, paid in the 1999–2000 school year, will increase year by year, depending on the average increase in tuition (normally 5 percent to 7 percent in Ohio).
5. Cincotta, personal correspondence, 12 December 1999.

chapter eleven

THE LAST RESORT

Chandra Brown was very young when she married her high school sweetheart. She often talked about how popular he was and what it was like to date the star wide receiver on the football team. "I thought I was so lucky to be dating Jerome. He was so popular and when I was with him, I felt like I was someone special," she once told her pastor, the Reverend Thomas Fry.

Unfortunately, as a young father, Jerome was not a star. After high school, Jerome had a hard time keeping a job and spent most evenings hanging around the local bars with his friends.

"Sometimes Jerome wouldn't come home at all. He knew that hurt me but, well, I guess he just didn't care," said Chandra rather shyly. "Then when he did come home smelling like alcohol, he would yell at me and push me around and even hit the boys sometimes," she continued as her eyes began to tear. "One night he left and he's never come back. No one knows where he is. The boys . . . oh, the boys are always hoping and praying that he'll come home again. But I don't think so. That was almost fourteen years ago."

Left to fend for her family alone, Chandra eventually passed her GED test, and, through the encouragement of Pastor Fry, she attended night school at the local community college in south Chicago. There she earned her associate of arts degree, and afterward she was able to get a job at one of Chicago's finest law firms. She road the "El" train to and from work during the hours her children were in school.

As her three sons grew older and started high school, Chandra extended her hours at the law firm. There she received a moderate salary and some minor benefits and soon became one of the firm's most respected legal assistants. Although Uncle Sam was not interested in her benefit package nor the growing medical bills for her children, he was definitely interested in her salary as it appeared on her son's financial aid application. As a single mother with three children, Chandra was disappointed when her oldest son, Anthony, received a notice from the university that he would only be eligible for a Stafford Loan.

When Anthony first received the notice from the university, Chandra began to do research concerning this government loan. She knew firsthand what it was like to live day to day and hoped her sons would not have to experience what she had gone through years before. She wondered whether the loan—or any loan—was the right way to go. Then, after hearing personal testimonies of former students and reading essays and data on the Internet, Chandra quickly concluded that the Stafford Loan program encouraged excessive borrowing.

PROVISIONS OF THE STAFFORD LOAN

Borrowing Levels

Depending on the student's expected family contribution, a student may receive subsidized Stafford Loans up to $65,500 and another $73,000 in unsubsidized Stafford Loans. *Subsidized* simply means that the government pays the interest while the student is in school and during the six-month grace period following graduation. Thus, once the student's total borrowing passes $65,500, the rest of the loan is subject to interest while in the classroom, effectively adding to the total balance upon graduation.

Banks, state governments, credit unions, and insurance companies funded the original Stafford Loans as part of the Federal Family Education Loan Program. After the federal government decided to help fund this educational loan, many of the original banks dropped out of the program. Today, most of the funds are disbursed by the U.S. Department of Education through the schools to the student as part of the William D. Ford Federal Direct Loan Program.

Dependent undergraduates may borrow $2,600 as freshmen, $3,500 as sophomores, and $5,500 per year thereafter up to $23,000. Thus a four-year student can borrow up to $17,100. To add to the dilemma, every student can borrow regardless of past credit problems. If the parents do qualify for the Parent Loan (described on page 117), any additional funds would be designated as unsubsidized and would accrue interest from the point of origination.

During graduate school the same student can borrow an additional amount of subsidized funds up to a max of $65,500 for his undergraduate and graduate education costs. If the student needs funds beyond that, he can borrow *unsubsidized* funds for graduate or professional school up to a maximum of $73,000. The limits are the same for students who are classified as independent.

If Anthony were to go on to graduate school, Chandra thought, *he could borrow as much as $138,000 and that would really put him into financial bondage. Why, that's more than I've made all my life!*

"Tell me," she once asked one of the law partners, "will the interest rates on those student loans go sky high if the economy changes?"

The Interest Rate and Origination Fee

"No, that's one good thing," answered her colleague. "In fact, from time to time the payback interest rate will go down based on the ninety-one-day Treasury bill. However, the maximum rate is still fixed at 8.25 percent."

Another partner who overheard the conversation interjected, "The unsubsidized Stafford Loan, Chandra, is nothing more than another government entitlement program open to all families, regardless of income and net worth. The interest accrues the entire time a student is in school, and even though you can pay the interest every quarter, most people just let it add up until they graduate. And you still have the 4 percent origination fee on every dollar like the loans that are subsidized.

"I know what I'm talking about," he continued. "I'm still paying off my student loans, and I've been practicing law for almost nine years. When my sister started college, my parents took out one of those expensive Parent Loans. I feel really bad for them. In fact, we don't talk about it. It's not a subject that anyone dares bring up whenever I go home to visit," he laughed.

"There were rumors for years, Chandra," he went on, "that the Stafford Loan would become service cancelable. Well, they finally did it, at least for teachers. I don't know if any of your boys want to become teachers, but if they do and they teach for five straight years, I understand that Uncle Sam will pick up the tab for $5,000 of their Stafford. That helps, but it's not a lot if you owe $80,000 or more."

Once qualified for the loan, students can easily obtain large sums, and, by paying only the minimum and having the interest accrue on the unsubsidized portion during school, graduate with a mountain of debt. I once knew a young doctor who owed what seemed like a fortune when she graduated, more than $92,000. She was overwhelmed with debt; once she told a patient that she would not be completely finished paying off her student loans until she was seventy years old.

RECENT HISTORY OF EDUCATIONAL LOANS

The legal partner was sharing a tale of woe that many participants in the student loan program could recite. During the last decade of the twentieth century, the federal government made it easy for college students to borrow massive amounts of money regardless of family income, which led to record-level borrowing. During that time, the Health Education Assistance Loan program was phased out and the Department of Education increased the overall loan limit on unsubsidized Stafford Loans for professional students. The new aggregate loan limit for those studying medicine, dentistry, podiatry, optometry, osteopathy, veterinary medicine, pharmacy, chiropractic, health administration, and clinical psychology is now $189,000, less any subsidized loans.

As previously noted, total borrowing is now above $50 billion, and the high level of funds available through the Stafford Loan has much to do with this level—and with the thousands of students in default on their student loans.

TOTAL COST OF THE STAFFORD LOAN

Borrowing federal Stafford Loans with a maximum interest rate of 8.25 percent can turn into a student's worst nightmare following graduation. Once students learn the *true cost,* they are more inclined to reject them. Since all Stafford Loans have a 4 percent origination fee, a typical $10,000 subsidized Stafford Loan will cost the student $400 for the privilege of borrowing the money plus the finance charge. When the 4 percent fee is added to repayment figures provided by the U.S. Department of Education, students could end up paying *more than double* the amount borrowed.

The table on the next page shows the sample costs for repaying a *subsidized* Stafford Loan. Should the loan be unsubsidized, the total cost and payments would be even greater than indicated. Interest on unsubsidized loans must either be paid quarterly while the student is in school or accrue and be added to the total cost of the loan at graduation. See appendix 11 for examples of costs in repaying loans ranging from $5,000 to $50,000.

TOTAL INTEREST & FEES FOR SUBSIDIZED
STAFFORD LOAN INCLUDING ORIGINATION FEES

Plan	Loan	Interest*	Monthly Payments	Actual Payback	Percentile†
10 yr.	$10,000	8.25%	$123.00	$15,118	51.2%
15 yr.	$10,000	8.25%	$ 97.00	$17,863	78.6%
20 yr.	$10,000	8.25%	$ 85.00	$20,850	108.5%

*This represents the maximum allowable rate. Depending on economic conditions, the interest rate may be lower.
†Percentile figures rounded and include 4 percent origination fee.

"Student loans themselves are not the problem," says Larry Burkett, founder and president of Christian Financial Concepts. "The problem is that students often borrow in excess of what they need to get a college education. A student loan should only be considered as the 'last resort.'"

THE DIRECT PARENT LOAN PROGRAM

The Direct Parent Loan for Undergraduate Students is set up exactly like the Direct Stafford Loan, with the Department of Education disbursing all funds through the school to the parents. The standard Parent Loan is still funded by banks, credit unions, and insurance companies. In most cases, repayment begins within sixty days of the loan origination unless the lender agrees to a deferment. Borrowers under the direct program have a choice of three repayment methods. The standard repayment plan requires a minimum of $50 per month up to ten years. The extended plan also has a minimum of $50 per month but up to thirty years. The graduated repayment plan allows for reduced payments followed by arbitrary increases every twenty-four months up to thirty years.

Significantly, there is no limit on the amount one can borrow. As long as the loan does not exceed the cost of education (less any other financial aid received by the student), parents can receive a loan while the student is in school, adding greatly to their debt.

That's one reason Chandra showed no interest in a Direct Parent Loan to help Anthony's education. "There is no limit," Chandra told one of her friends. "Parents can just go on and on and borrow whatever they want!" she exclaimed.

The interest on the Parent Loan is considerably higher than the Stafford Loan, based on the fifty-two week T-Bill, plus 3.1 percent adjusted annually, not to exceed 9 percent. Like the Stafford, there is also a 4 percent fee deducted from each disbursement. In addition, the Parent Loan is not service cancelable and may only be discharged for death or permanent and total disability, or if the student for whom the parent borrowed the loan should die.

NEGOTIATING THE FUNDING ARRANGEMENTS

As schools mail their award letters in the spring or summer, many parents are shocked, like Chandra Brown, to see their student's financial aid package bursting with Stafford Loans. If parents find this funding arrangement unacceptable, they can certainly meet with the school financial aid department to discuss the decision. However, the student and parents should make an appointment to meet *in person* with the *head* of the financial aid department. Having a personal face-to-face meeting does two things. First, it gives both the student and parents an opportunity to begin building a relationship with the financial aid administrator; and second, it allows parents a platform to present any unusual expenses that may not have been picked up by the financial aid form. Financial aid should never be negotiated over the telephone.

Anthony always had his heart set on attending a Big Ten university, and after calling to make an appointment, he and his mother met with the financial aid staff at the school. He knew it was important to make a good impression on everyone and wore one of his best suits. "He even wore a tie," said Chandra, "and he hates ties!"

"We go strictly by the income and asset data as indicated on your son's Student Aid Report, Ms. Brown," said the financial aid administrator. "If there are errors or unusual or special circumstances, we are always glad to review the report," he added.

He examined carefully all the factors related to Anthony's federal application, including the large medical bills the family faced with Anthony's younger brother. The administrator concluded Anthony could qualify for more funding; he arranged for a small Pell Grant, a Perkins Loan, and even a work-study job as a tutor helping inner-city kids learn how to read through the government's "America Reads Challenge."

While a financial aid administrator cannot arbitrarily change a student's expected family contribution, the administrator may make a professional judgment and adjust the components that determine the contribution at his or her discretion based on unusual circumstances.

Since the amount of nonrepayable grants versus repayable loans differs widely from school to school, many parents and students shop schools for the best financial aid package. They reason that if one school offers a better aid package than another, the competing school may make a favorable counter offer. Some colleges, especially private schools, are very competitive and will negotiate; others will not and may be offended at the suggestion.

With the heavy increase of student loans, Uncle Sam has added an additional repayment clause that allows students to receive forbearance for up to three years if their student loan debt is greater than 20 percent of their income.

Under special conditions, some students may be eligible for loan deferments. Excluding the Parent Loan, the interest may also be deferred if the borrower is pursuing at least a half-time course of study, is enrolled in a graduate fellowship program, including those outside the country, or is disabled and in rehabilitation training.

Students with diverse loans (Perkins, Stafford, PLUS, HPSL, or HEAL) totaling more than $7,500 may consolidate their loans even if the loans are delinquent or in default. However, I do not recommend loan consolidation because it severely lengthens the years for students to become debt free.

The wise parent will remember Larry Burkett's advice and consider a student loan only as the "last resort." At times, a loan may be necessary, but it should be a small amount and, ideally, will not be needed every year the student is in school. By limiting the amount of student loan borrowing, both parents and their child will feel a great sense of financial freedom on the student's graduation day.

chapter twelve

ABOUT DISTANCE EDUCATION

T hey finally came up with a solution. Now I can stay logged on and you can still talk on the telephone," Brenda Ferguson told her roommate, Teresa.

"How can we do that? I thought every time we even received a call, it knocked us off-line," commented Teresa.

"I don't know exactly how it works," explained Brenda, "but it's this thing called DSL and the technician told me we can talk and fax and be on the Internet all at the same time and still not lose the connection."

A DSL (Digital Subscriber Line) empowers a person on the computer to download files off the Internet more than one hundred times faster than the newest analog modems. It is especially helpful for the thousands of students like Brenda who need to stayed connected at all times in order to complete their college classes online. Indeed, on-line higher education is being offered by more and more schools and is a way to attend a "college without walls" and graduate with an academic degree from an accredited school.

Brenda Ferguson grew up in the Northeast where both her parents worked in shoe factories. Neither her parents nor her two brothers completed the twelfth grade, so when Brenda graduated from high school and started taking classes at a community college, her parents were delighted. A year later, Brenda transferred to a state university but struggled trying to keep a balance between classes and her work schedule. After only one year, Brenda dropped out of college.

But seven years later, she realized that her job was at a dead end. She had worked in the same position for five years and always had the feeling that she had been passed over for a promotion simply because she didn't have a degree. Once she received all the information concerning distance education, Brenda made an appointment to meet with the head of the company's human resource department and asked to be considered for employer-paid tuition assistance. Although this kind of employee benefit is normally reserved for those attending graduate school, much to her surprise, Brenda learned within a week that her request had been granted.

With her new DSL and a borrowed computer, Brenda was able to return to college and actively participate in real-time video conferencing with her professors and other students using the same phone line. "The best thing about the digital connection," Brenda told her friends, "is that it's always on. I don't have to wait to get started or have delays because of busy signals."

THE GROWTH OF DISTANCE EDUCATION

When the terms *Internet* and *worldwide web* became household words in the late 1990s, off-campus education received a new lease on life and a new name, *Distance Education*. Distance education is not new; correspondence schools have been part of the educational landscape in the United States for decades. What is new is the manner in which it is treated and accepted by educators. In its latest electronic form, distance education allows students to attend classes at major universities around the country and even receive a bachelor's or master's degree without ever stepping foot on campus. Predictions are that distance learning will graduate as many as 15 percent of all students by 2010.

The incredible growth of distance education continues to amaze even the most conservative of educators. Some are predicting that within the next decade, 25 percent of all graduate courses will be available on the Internet. "You may have more virtual options than ever before," wrote Pam Dixon, author of *Virtual College*. "Even stodgy universities that have traditionally snubbed distance education are jumping on the virtual bandwagon."[1]

"With the onslaught of electronic communication, distance education is no longer distant," said Charlotte Thomas, career and education editor at Peterson's publishing. "Technology has irrevocably altered the relationship between student and professor and even what is considered a classroom situation. [Unfortunately] federal and state regulations have not kept pace."[2]

THE TYPICAL DISTANCE LEARNER

Those generating excitement for distance learners include corporate America, government agencies, and even military installations, all of whom view distance learning as a means to educate key people without losing them for hours or weeks at a time to on-campus study. As a result, many students are now receiving employer-paid tuition reimbursement as they earn their bachelor's or master's degree on-line. (For more information on employer-paid tuition reimbursement, review page 81.)

In some ways, distance learners are unique. Many have jobs and families. Most are over twenty-five years of age, predominately female, highly motivated, and exceptionally determined to complete their education.[3] As an example, Auburn University (www.auburn.edu) allows on-line students five years to complete their MBA program, but most finish in three years or less.

This older-student profile raises a legitimate question: What about a student who just graduated from high school and has always had close one-on-one contact with teachers and other students? Can that person survive in the hands-off environment at a virtual university? Some educators are skeptical and suggest that students first participate in a traditional on-campus setting, such as a community college. The discipline and challenge of college learning often can be better developed for younger students by being on-site.

On the other hand, many younger students with maturity may welcome the freedom to interact electronically with college professors and others students at the virtual level. They will still interact with their professors and other college students, although they will not have the so-called total college experience that includes extracurricular activities and other social opportunities found on campus. The ability to reduce overall college expenses combined with a student's maturity probably will be the determining factors.

Those who venture into the world of education at a distance "must be fairly self-directed and conscientious about completing assignments to succeed in a distance-delivered class," warned Ed Neal in *Phi Kappa Phi Journal*. "Most still require ample and timely feedback on their performance. The demands that distance learning places on the learner make it unlikely that the vast majority of traditional-age college students will be able to succeed under this mode of instruction."[4]

PARTICIPATING COLLEGES AND UNIVERSITIES

As for geographical boundaries, there are very few. For example, at Georgia Institute of Technology (www.gatech.edu), students from all over the world can now study and receive a master of science degree in electrical engineering. More than nine hundred students were enrolled in distance education at Georgia Tech in 1999. Similar figures can be found across the country. The University of Phoenix (http://online.uophx.edu) now enrolls nearly 60,000 students, of which over 7,000 students are taking courses exclusively on-line. The University of Dallas (http://home1.gte.net/cfdl) now has an on-line student population representing fifty countries. Stanford University (www-scpd.Stanford.edu) offers an on-line degree in engineering reachable from every area of the world, and the Graduate School of Management at the California Virtual University (www.california.edu) boasts nearly 30,000 students on-line, mostly working adults with jobs and families. The web site features information on undergraduate schools and on-line courses from scores of institutions of higher education in California, including hundreds of courses available from the California State Colleges, the University of California, the state's community colleges plus seventy-one private schools.

Both Endicott College in Endicott, Massachusetts, and the University of Maryland University College in College Park, Maryland, offer on-line degrees, and both offer students the opportunity to earn college credits based on work and life experience. This alone can save the distance learner hundreds or even thousands of dollars in tuition costs.

Endicott College is linked to NewPromise.com, allowing degree candidates to complete their entire program of study through Endicott College. Following the completion of an academic career assessment, students are provided a recommended study program and given the opportunity to select from hundreds of courses available from over fifteen hundred fully accredited colleges and universities available through www.NewPromise.com.

Furthermore, students enrolled at Endicott College may petition for up to thirty proficiency credits for work and life experience. Even students without any college history can take entry-level courses and earn their degree through "EC Online" at www.endicott.edu.

The University of Maryland University College at www.umuc.edu/bdaad offered its first distance-education courses in 1972. Today, UMUC fosters a highly successful program entitled "Bachelor's Degree at a Distance" with enrollment around the world. Through their EXCEL program, distance learners may apply for up to thirty academic credits toward their undergraduate degree in one of two ways: credit for previous work and life experience and/or college credits by examination.

In addition, UMUC has a cooperative education program whereby degree candidates can also earn up to fifteen upper-level course credits toward their bachelor's degree through their co-op employment.

Most schools, including the above, are accredited. Accreditation of the school is very important, for it assures the recognition and transfer of academic credits to other schools. Later we will explore accreditation further in the section, "Questions for Prospective Students to Ask." Here is a partial list of other notable accredited schools on-line:

Colorado State University (www.colostate.edu)

Columbia University (www.cvn.columbia.edu)

Duke University (www.fuqua.duke.edu)

Golden State University (http://cybercampus.ggu.edu/)

Iowa State University (www.iastate.edu)

Stephens College (www.stephens.edu)

Syracuse University (www.suce.syr.edu)

University of Arizona (www.sir.arizona.edu)

University of Colorado, (www.colorado.edu)

University of Massachusetts, (www.umass.edu)

Washington State University (www.eus.wsu.edu)

ADJUSTMENTS AND ADVANTAGES TO DISTANCE EDUCATION

Adjustments

It was not easy for Brenda when she first started back to school to earn her bachelor's degree. It had been seven years since she had even looked at a college textbook, and, like many returning students, Brenda was apprehensive about studying at a distance. Nevertheless, she wrote her high school principal requesting that transcripts be sent to her new on-line admissions office. She also provided the school with a copy of a transcript and her grades at the state university she had attended years before.

"I thought it was going to be a big hassle trying to get accepted at the new college," Brenda told Teresa. "I was so surprised! They actually made me feel comfortable, you know, like they wanted me. And then, can you believe this? Human resources even said I could bring home one of the extra laptops we have at work and work here on the Internet."

Advantages

But some adjustments were easier, thanks to modern technology. Brenda did not enter a classroom, yet she could confer with professors and other students.

Like all on-line students, she needed a fax machine, color television for video conferencing, a videocassette recorder, and voice mail to stay in touch with her professors and classmates. To complete the distance-education connection, Brenda needed a computer with a fast modem, a high-speed CD-ROM drive, and Internet and E-mail connections for daily assignments.

Some educators agree that distance learning may be more stimulating and even encourage more critical reasoning than traditional large lecture classes, because of the interaction that takes place in small-group settings. A study by sociology professor Jerald Schutte found that test scores for both midterm and final examinations were on average 20 percent higher for those taking classes on-line versus students taking the very same subject in a traditional classroom.[5] In a different study published by www.eCollege.com, 85 percent of the faculty respondents said their students learned equally effectively on-line as on campus, and some indicated that their students did even better.

New Forms of the Virtual Classroom

This may help explain why hundreds of students are enrolling in America's first fully accredited virtual institution, Jones International University (JIU). JIU has no campus, no impressive buildings, and no student union where students may congregate. Instead, the school promises to deliver a virtual classroom electronically to participants wherever they live via the Internet and worldwide web. The school received formal accreditation in 1999 from the North Central Association of Colleges and Schools, a major regional accrediting agency of schools of higher education. JIU offers both bachelor of arts and master of arts degrees in business communication.[6]

Another method for awarding certificates and degrees was developed by the planning board for Western Governors University (WGU). The governors of fifteen western states and one U.S. territory founded the virtual institution with a vision of making higher education more accessible. Thousands of courses are available through WGU from hundreds of participating schools. Based on knowledge of a particular subject, a student can earn a degree or certificate by demonstrating a superior grasp of that subject through a WGU assessment. Instead of being credit-based, Western Governors University is a competency-based institution. More information may be found at www.wgu.edu.

In *Distance Degrees,* Mark Wilson notes that both Regents College (www.regents.edu) and Thomas Edison State College in New Jersey (www.tesc.edu) will grant a bachelor's degree based solely on credits earned from passing equivalency examinations and/or from life experience.

Application and Acceptance

Students applying for admission into one of the hundreds of virtual or distance-education institutions will find it no different from applying for admittance to a traditional college or university. Applications, essays, and SAT/ACT scores will still be required for those without any prior college history.

For those going "back" to college on-line, it's usually a matter of having a transcript from a previous college sent to the on-line school. For those returning, it could mean as few as ten to twenty credit hours to complete their degree. Those seeking an advanced graduate degree are usually required to take the GRE (Graduate Record Exam) or the GMAT (Graduate Management Admission Test) prior to admittance.

THE "CLASSROOM" EXPERIENCE

Homework and Exams

Some things never change. Once accepted, there is always the question of homework. Students who didn't like homework in high school or in a previous college setting probably won't like the homework administered by professors from a distance. It's principally the same. The same type of research is required, the same book reports are due, and the same papers need to be penned. The only difference is in the delivery methods employed.

Other questions students frequently ask concern taking tests and the actual interaction among professors and students. Testing for distance learners is normally done using an assigned proctor to oversee the test. If the student is employed while studying at a distance, the proctor may be the student's supervisor or manager. Very often, the virtual school will designate an overseer located in a local community college. By controlling the testing procedures, the schools involved are able to maintain standards equal to their counterparts.

INTERACTION BETWEEN PROFESSORS AND STUDENTS

To assure a fair grade, most distance professors employ a mix of written assignments, tests, and class participation. Many expect increased participation from on-line students during videoconferencing segments. While the video portion is normally one-way, the audio portion is a two-way connection and allows everyone to ask questions and make statements. This is normally done using a speakerphone where the instructor, other on-line students, and those in the classroom (where the live broadcast originates) can all hear the comments and questions and respond directly.

Today, with the expansion of network computing and two-way video, distance education is rapidly becoming more like a traditional classroom with face-to-face interaction. Then, too, many assignments are purposely designated as team projects, forcing on-line students to actively participate with other on-line students via telephone and E-mail and interact directly with the teacher.

Schools employ a variety of means to deliver course work to a student's virtual classroom, including videocassettes, E-mail, the electronic bulletin board, audiocassettes, CD-ROMs, audioconferencing, and cable- or satellite-directed videoconferencing.

For everyone in Brenda Ferguson's on-line class, one distance education course was regularly scheduled every Tuesday and Wednesday at 7:30 P.M. via a satellite connection. For some students, there may not be a set meeting time. They simply download course material from the Internet and discuss the contents via E-mail. For example, CyberEd (a term that describes the University of Massachusetts Dartmouth Division of Continuing Education) delivers virtual courses through the worldwide web and E-mail. Courses are structured around the teachers' weekly assignments, and students participate in class through message boards and other electronic means. According to CyberEd literature, there is no set time when students must be at their computers, allowing greater flexibility for both students and teachers.

QUESTIONS FOR PROSPECTIVE STUDENTS TO ASK

Key Questions

For most students studying on-line, time is a major factor, as it was for Brenda. Before filling out an application on-line or via the postal service, students should ask a number of direct questions. Here are four major questions to ask: (1) Is the school fully accredited, and if so, by whose authority? (2) What is the cost per credit unit compared to the costs at traditional schools for the same program? (3) How long does it take to complete each course or program, and by what means is the course-work delivered? (4) Does the school accept transfer credits from other distance-learning institutions, and do the programs offered meet the federal government's guidelines for student financial aid?

Two other key questions would be: (1) What percent of the faculty hold a doctoral degree? (2) Do the professors have regular office hours for teacher-student phone conferences? Students should also ask the logistical questions. Are textbooks available on-line or do they need to be purchased locally? When special software is required to be loaded on the student's own computer, does the school provide specialized software training prior to any course delivery?

QUESTIONS ABOUT ACCREDITATION

It is critical for all prospective students to verify that either the federal government or the Council for Higher Education Accreditation accredits the school offering a distance education. Such accreditation gives credibility when applying for a job and a greater likelihood of college course approval when transferring to another school. However, when transferring, remember that the receiving school can choose to accept or reject incoming course credits from another college, regardless of accreditation.

As more educational institutions are accredited, students are becoming increasingly interested in the multiplicity of courses and degrees available on-line. As noted earlier, most distance-learning schools are accredited, and often are extensions of well-know colleges and universities. However, as Mark Wilson warned in *Distance Degrees,* "Don't get pulled in by one of those sham operators. There are illegal schools that essentially sell worthless paper [degrees]."

If in doubt, students should ask to see a copy of the school's official accreditation. For a complete listing of the regional accreditation agencies, including the states they represent, see: www.ed.gov/offices/OPE/students/file4a.html.

The U.S. Department of Education also recognizes the DETC (Distance Education and Training Council), which publishes a list of schools they endorse nationwide. Some of the institutions accredited by the DETC include schools that offer courses in airline/travel at www.iatac.com, a diploma in landscaping, flower arrangement, or dressmaking at www.lifetime-career.com, a diploma as a paralegal at www.nipas.net, or a certificate for interior design at www.rhodec.com. Other students may venture out and study to be a graduate gemologist at www.gia.edu, earn a master of science in financial planning at www.fp.edu, a bachelor of science in health services/management at www.cchs.edu, a master's degree in military science at www.amunet.edu, or a bachelor of science in criminal justice at www.aju.edu. For a complete listing, call the Distance Education and Training Council at 202-234-5100.

AVAILABLE FINANCIAL AID

As distance education continues to grow as an educational option, both schools and students are calling for more flexibility in the area of financial aid. In the past, financial aid has always determined by the number of hours a student physically sat in a classroom in a recognized facility.

The financial aid picture continues to change annually, and distance-education students may find Pell Grants and Federal Perkins Loans available at the time of application. As more students break from traditional on-campus classrooms to the nontraditional "laptop classroom," the Department of Education is actively pursuing changes concerning financial aid at both the administrative level and on Capitol Hill.

For example, based on the Higher Education Act (as of early 2000), students enrolled at institutions that offer more than 50 percent of their courses via distance education are not eligible for federal student aid. However, the demand for student financial aid is forcing regulators to take another look at what used to be considered just correspondence courses. In 1999 Education Secretary Richard W. Riley announced in a department press release: "Recent advances in technology and use of the Internet have resulted in a spectacular growth in distance education and present us with a twofold challenge: to ensure that students pursuing high-quality distance learning programs have access to federal student aid and, at the same time, to ensure the integrity of the federal student aid programs."

Later that year the department established the Distance Education Demonstration Program. For those colleges, systems, and consortia participating in the program (and only those schools), the department waived two major legislative obstacles prohibiting federal financial aid. Included was the restriction concerning the number of weeks a student must be enrolled to receive federal aid and the restriction prohibiting student aid at those institutions offering more than 50 percent of their classes at a distance.

The purpose behind the Demonstration Program is to ensure the integrity of the federal student aid programs while testing new methods for delivering federal aid to distance-education students.

Those participating in the distance-education research project in 1999 consisted of 117 institutions, including Western Governors University, Florida State University, Southern Christian University, New York University, and the University of Maryland University College. A complete listing of the participants in the Distance Education Demonstration Program can be found at: www.ed.gov/PressReleases/06-1999/distep.html.

Many believe that distance education is a win-win situation for everyone. Distance learners can save money while getting an education from almost anywhere in the world, and the colleges and universities benefit by increasing their overall student population and tuition income without having to spend millions on new buildings.

NOTES

1. Pam Dixon, *Virtual College* (Princeton, N. J.: Peterson's, 1996), 15.
2. Petersons on-line, on the Internet at www.petersons.com/dlearn/who.html; accessed on 23 February 2000.
3. Ibid.
4. Ed Neal, "Distance Education," *Phi Kappa Phi Journal* 79 (Winter 1999): 40.
5. Jerald G. Schutte, "Virtual Teaching in Higher Education," academic article cited on the Internet at www.csun.edu/sociology/virexp.htm; accessed 24 February 2000.
6. For more information on earning a bachelor's or master's degree at Jones International, call 888-811-5663 or log on to: www.jonesinternational.edu.

FINANCIAL AID VERSUS COSTS

PROJECTED SOURCES OF FUTURE FINANCIAL AID

A total of approximately $75 billion in financial aid for higher education is projected to be available for the school year 2001–02.

Source	Percent Amount of total	Amount in billions
Private Resources	1%	$8
VA Benefits	1.5	1.3
Employer-Paid Benefits	3	2.8
State-Provided Assistance	5	4
Tuition Tax Credits	7	6.1
Government Grants	13	11.5
College Resources	17	14.9
Government Loans	52	46.2

FUTURE COLLEGE COSTS

The following projections include the costs of tuition, room, board, books, travel, and living expenses. The cost indicated for the two year public (community) college reflects only tuition and books. Each estimate is for one year of college.

SCHOOL	2001/02	2002/03	2003/04	2004/05	2005/06
4-Yr Private	$29,800	$31,000	$31,800	$33,700	$35,100
4-Yr Public	14,900	15,500	16,500	17,300	18,000
2-Yr Public	2,750	2,950	3,225	3,600	3,720

Source: Adapted from "Planning for College," a brochure from Met Life Resources of Metropolitan Life Insurance Co., 1996. The figures have been adjusted for inflationary factors.

CAREER OPPORTUNITIES

Guided by a student's interests and aptitude, a high school guidance counselor can assist in directing the student to the college that will best fit his or her career objective. The U.S. Department of Education has listed the following levels of higher education needed to prepare for the specific careers shown.

Two–Year College (Associate's Degree)	Four–Year College (Bachelor's Degree)	Four–Plus Years (Graduate's Degree)
Computer technician	Teacher	Lawyer
Surveyor	Accountant	Doctor
Registered nurse	FBI special agent	Dentist
Dental hygienist	Engineer	Architect
Medical lab technician	Journalist	Registered dietitian
Commercial artist	Insurance agent	Psychologist
Restaurant manager	Investment banker	Minister
Engineering technician	Graphic designer	Veterinarian
Auto mechanic	Public relations	Geologist
Administrative assistant	Writer	College professor
Plant operator	Advertising agent	Economist
Heating, refrigeration, A. C. technician	Zoologist	

COLLEGE APPLICATION CHECKLIST

The following checklist can help parents and students keep track when meeting the requirements of specific colleges to which they seek admission. Feel free to make copies of this list, one for each college.

College _____

Date Application Requested _____ Date Application Received _____

Application Deadline

Does the student seek an early action/early decision, or is this a regular admission?

Early Decision Date _____ Regular Decision Date _____

Standardized Testing

SAT I   ACT   (circle one)   Date Sent _____

SAT II Scores?

Circle one: Required   Recommended   Not Required   Date Sent _____

Interview

Circle one: Required   Recommended   Not Required Date Completed _____

Application Completed

General Portion   Date Sent _____

Essays:

         Essay 1   Date Sent _____

         Essay 2   Date Sent _____

Transcripts   Date Requested _____ Date Received _____

Teacher Recommendations

         Recommendation 1   Date Requested _____

         Recommendation 2   Date Requested _____

Other Recommendation Letters

Circle one: Permitted   Not Permitted   Requested   Date Sent _____

Confirmation Received? (circle one)   Yes   No

                                          Date Received _____

                                          Date Notified _____

appendix four

SAMPLE FAFSA AND PROFILE FORMS

Most colleges and universities want all incoming students requesting financial aid, whether home-schooled or schooled in a private or public school, to file the FAFSA. The preprinted copy is reproduced on the following pages as an introduction to the procedure and requirements. The FAFSA accounts for some ten million financial aid forms processed annually.

Some institutions also require the student to complete the financial aid profile of the College Scholarship Service, known as the CSS/Financial Aid PROFILE. A sample PROFILE form follows the FAFSA.

Please recognize that these are sample forms; do not fill out or mail the following samples. Official FAFSA and PROFILE forms are available from college financial aid offices and in most high schools. Forms need to be mailed after January 1 of the award year in order to provide current income, assets, and tax figures.

NOTE: SAMPLE ONLY

Free Application for Federal Student Aid
OMB 1845-0001   *July 1, 2000 — June 30, 2001 school year*

Step One: For questions 1-36, leave blank any questions that do not apply to you (the student).

1-3. Your full name (as it appears on your Social Security card)

1. LAST NAME: F O R   I N F O R M A T I O N   O N L Y
2. FIRST NAME: D O   N O T   S U B M I T
3. M.I.

4-7. Your permanent mailing address

4. NUMBER AND STREET (INCLUDE APARTMENT NUMBER)

5. CITY (AND COUNTRY, IF NOT U.S.)   6. STATE   7. ZIP CODE

8. Your Social Security Number
X X X – X X – X X X X

9. Your date of birth
MONTH / DAY / YEAR 1 9

10. Your permanent telephone number
AREA CODE

11. Do you have a driver's license?   Yes ○ 1   No ○ 2

12-13. Driver's license number and state
12. LICENSE NUMBER   13. STATE

14. Are you a U.S. citizen? Pick one. **See Page 2.**
a. Yes, I am a U.S. citizen. .... ○ 1
b. No, but I am an eligible noncitizen. **Fill in question 15.** ○ 2
c. No, I am not a citizen or eligible noncitizen. .... ○ 3

15. ALIEN REGISTRATION NUMBER   A

16. Marital status as of today
I am single, divorced, or widowed. ○ 1
I am married. ○ 2
I am separated. ○ 3

17. Month and year you were married, separated, divorced, or widowed
MONTH / YEAR

For each question (18 - 22), please mark whether you will be full time, 3/4 time, half time, less than half time, or not attending. Mark "Full time" if you are not sure. See page 2.

	Full time	3/4 time	Half time	Less than half time	Not attending
18. Summer 2000	○ 1	○ 2	○ 3	○ 4	○ 5
19. Fall semester or quarter 2000	○ 1	○ 2	○ 3	○ 4	○ 5
20. Winter quarter 2000-2001	○ 1	○ 2	○ 3	○ 4	○ 5
21. Spring semester or quarter 2001	○ 1	○ 2	○ 3	○ 4	○ 5
22. Summer 2001	○ 1	○ 2	○ 3	○ 4	○ 5

	Middle school/Jr. High	High school	College or beyond	Other/unknown
23. Highest school your father completed	○ 1	○ 2	○ 3	○ 4
24. Highest school your mother completed	○ 1	○ 2	○ 3	○ 4

25. What is your state of legal residence?   STATE

26. Did you become a legal resident of this state before January 1, 1995?   Yes ○ 1   No ○ 2

27. If the answer to question 26 is **"No,"** give month and year you became a legal resident.
MONTH / YEAR

28. If you have **never** been convicted of any illegal drug offense, enter "1" in the box and go to question 29. A drug-related conviction does not necessarily make you ineligible for aid; call 1-800-433-3243 or go to http://www.fafsa.ed.gov/q28 to find out how to fill out this question.

29. Most male students must register with Selective Service to get federal aid. Are you male?   Yes ○ 1   No ○ 2

30. If you are male (age 18-25) and not registered, do you want Selective Service to register you?   Yes ○ 1   No ○ 2

31. What degree or certificate will you be working towards during 2000-2001? **See page 2** and enter the correct number in the box.

32. What will be your grade level when you begin the 2000-2001 school year? **See page 2** and enter the correct number in the box.

33. Will you have a high school diploma or GED before you enroll?   Yes ○ 1   No ○ 2

34. Will you have your first bachelor's degree before July 1, 2000?   Yes ○ 1   No ○ 2

35. In addition to grants, are you interested in student loans (which you must pay back)?   Yes ○ 1   No ○ 2

36. In addition to grants, are you interested in "work-study" (which you earn through work)?   Yes ○ 1   No ○ 2

Step Two: For 37-51, if you (the student) are now married (even if you were not married in 1999), report both your and your spouse's income and assets. Ignore references to "spouse" if you are currently single, separated, divorced, or widowed.

37. For 1999, have you filed your IRS income tax return or another tax return listed in **question 38**?

   a. I have already filed. ○ 1   **b.** I will file, but I have not yet filed. ○ 2   **c.** I'm not going to file. **(Skip to question 44.)** ○ 3

38. What income tax return did you file or will you file for 1999?

   a. IRS 1040 .... ○ 1   **c.** A foreign tax return. **See Page 2.** .... ○ 3

   b. IRS 1040A, 1040EZ, 1040Telefile ...... ○ 2   **d.** A tax return for Puerto Rico, Guam, American Samoa, the Virgin Islands, the Marshall Islands, the Federated States of Micronesia, or Palau. **See Page 2.** ...... ○ 4

39. If you have filed or will file a 1040, were you eligible to file a 1040A or 1040EZ? **See page 2.**   Yes ○ 1 No/don't know ○ 2

For questions 40-53, if the answer is zero or the question does not apply to you, enter 0.

40. What was your (and spouse's) adjusted gross income for 1999? Adjusted gross income is on IRS Form 1040–line 33; 1040A–line 18; 1040EZ–line 4; or Telefile–line I. $ ☐☐☐ , ☐☐☐

41. Enter the total amount of your (and spouse's) income tax for 1999. Income tax amount is on IRS Form 1040–line 49 plus 51; 1040A–line 32; 1040EZ–line 10; or Telefile–line K. $ ☐☐ , ☐☐☐

42. Enter your (and spouse's) exemptions. Exemptions are on IRS Form 1040–line 6d, or on Form 1040A–line 6d. For Form 1040EZ or Telefile, **see page 2.**   ☐☐

43. Enter your Earned Income Credit from IRS Form 1040–line 59a; 1040A–line 37a; 1040EZ–line 8a; or Telefile–line L. $ ☐☐☐ , ☐☐☐

44-45. How much did you (and spouse) earn from working in 1999? Answer this question whether or not you filed a tax return. This information may be on your W-2 forms, or on IRS Form 1040–lines 7, 12, and 18; 1040A–line 7; or 1040EZ–line 1. Telefilers should use their W-2's.   **You (44)** $ ☐☐☐ , ☐☐☐   **Your Spouse (45)** $ ☐☐☐ , ☐☐☐

46. Go to page 8 of this form; complete the column on the left of **Worksheet A**; enter student total here. $ ☐☐☐ , ☐☐☐

47. Go to page 8 of this form; complete the column on the left of **Worksheet B**; enter student total here. $ ☐☐☐ , ☐☐☐

48. Total current balance of cash, savings, and checking accounts $ ☐☐☐ , ☐☐☐

For 49-51, if net worth is one million or more, enter $999,999. If net worth is negative, enter 0.

49. Current net worth of investments (investment value minus investment debt) **See page 2.** $ ☐☐☐ , ☐☐☐

50. Current net worth of business (business value minus business debt) **See page 2.** $ ☐☐☐ , ☐☐☐

51. Current net worth of investment farm (Don't include a farm that you live on and operate.) $ ☐☐☐ , ☐☐☐

52-53. If you receive veterans education benefits, for **how many months** from July 1, 2000 through June 30, 2001 will you receive these benefits, and **what amount** will you receive per month? Do not include your spouse's veterans education benefits.   **Months (52)** ☐☐   **Amount (53)** $ ☐☐☐

Step Three: Answer all six questions in this step.

54. Were you born before January 1, 1977? .... Yes ○ 1 No ○ 2

55. Will you be working on a degree beyond a bachelor's degree in school year 2000-2001? .... Yes ○ 1 No ○ 2

56. As of today, are you married? (Answer yes if you are separated, but not divorced.) .... Yes ○ 1 No ○ 2

57. Answer **"Yes"** if: (1) You have children who receive more than half of their support from you; **or**
           (2) You have dependents (other than your children or spouse) who live with you and receive more than half of their support from you, now and through June 30, 2001. ... Yes ○ 1 No ○ 2

58. Are you an orphan or ward of the court or were you a ward of the court until age 18? .... Yes ○ 1 No ○ 2

59. Are you a veteran of the U.S. Armed Forces? **See page 2.** .... Yes ○ 1 No ○ 2

If you (the student) answer "No" to every question in Step Three, go to Step Four.

If you answer "Yes" to any question in Step Three, skip Step Four and go to Step Five.

(If you are a graduate health profession student, you may be required to complete Step Four even if you answered "Yes" to any question in Step Three.)

Step Four: Complete this step if you (the student) answered "No" to all questions in Step Three. Please tell us about your parents. **See page 7 for who is considered a parent.**

60. Parents' marital status as of today? (Pick one.)　Married ○ 1　Single ○ 2　Divorced/Separated ○ 3　Widowed ○ 4

61-62. Your father's Social Security Number and last name
- 61. FATHER'S/STEPFATHER'S SSN
- 62. FATHER'S/STEPFATHER'S LAST NAME

63-64. Your mother's Social Security Number and last name
- 63. MOTHER'S/STEPMOTHER'S SSN
- 64. MOTHER'S/STEPMOTHER'S LAST NAME

65. How many people are in your <u>parents' household</u>? **See page 7.**

66. How many in question 65 **(exclude your parents)** will be <u>college students</u> between July 1, 2000, and June 30, 2001? **See page 7.**

67. What is your parents' state of legal residence?　STATE

68. Did your parents become legal residents of the state in question 67 before January 1, 1995?　Yes ○ 1　No ○ 2

69. If the answer to question 68 is "No," give the month and year legal residency began for the parent who has lived in the state the longest.　MONTH / YEAR

70. What is the age of your older parent?

71. For 1999, have your parents filed their IRS income tax return or another tax return listed in **question 72**?
- **a.** My parents have already filed. ○ 1
- **b.** My parents will file, but they have not yet filed. ○ 2
- **c.** My parents are not going to file. **(Skip to question 78.)** ○ 3

72. What income tax return did your parents file or will they file for 1999?
- **a.** IRS 1040 .... ○ 1
- **b.** IRS 1040A, 1040EZ, 1040Telefile ..... ○ 2
- **c.** A foreign tax return. **See Page 2.** .... ○ 3
- **d.** A tax return for Puerto Rico, Guam, American Samoa, the Virgin Islands, the Marshall Islands, the Federated States of Micronesia, or Palau. **See Page 2** ...... ○ 4

73. If your parents have filed or will file a 1040, were they <u>eligible to file a 1040A or 1040EZ</u>? **See page 2.**　Yes ○ 1　No/don't know ○ 2

For 74 - 85, if the answer is zero or the question does not apply, enter 0.

74. What was your parents' adjusted gross income for 1999? Adjusted gross income is on IRS Form 1040–line 33; 1040A–line 18; 1040EZ–line 4; or Telefile–line I.　$ ___ , ___

75. Enter the total amount of your parents' income tax for 1999. Income tax amount is on IRS Form 1040–line 49 plus 51; 1040A–line 32; 1040EZ–line 10; or Telefile–line K.　$ ___ , ___

76. Enter your parents' exemptions. Exemptions are on IRS Form 1040–line 6d or on Form 1040A–line 6d. For Form 1040EZ or Telefile, **see page 2.**　___

77. Enter your parents' Earned Income Credit from IRS Form 1040–line 59a; 1040A–line 37a; 1040EZ–line 8a; or Telefile–line L.　$ ___ , ___

78-79. How much did your parents earn from working in 1999? Answer this question whether or not your parents filed a tax return. This information may be on their W-2 forms, or on IRS Form 1040–lines 7, 12, and 18; 1040A–line 7; or 1040EZ–line 1. Telefilers should use their W-2's.　**Father/ Stepfather (78)** $ ___ , ___　**Mother/ Stepmother (79)** $ ___ , ___

80. Go to page 8 of this form; complete the column on the right of **Worksheet A**; enter parent total here.　$ ___ , ___

81. Go to page 8 of this form; complete the column on the right of **Worksheet B**; enter parent total here.　$ ___ , ___

82. Total current balance of cash, savings, and checking accounts　$ ___ , ___

For 83–85, if net worth is one million or more, enter $999,999. If net worth is negative, enter 0.

83. Current <u>net worth</u> of <u>investments</u> (<u>investment value</u> minus <u>investment debt</u>) See page 2.　$ ___ , ___

84. Current <u>net worth</u> of business (<u>business value</u> minus <u>business debt</u>) **See page 2.**　$ ___ , ___

85. Current <u>net worth</u> of investment farm (Don't include a farm that your parents live on and operate.)　$ ___ , ___

Now go to Step Six.

Step Five: Complete this step only if you (the student) answered "Yes" to any question in Step Three.

86. How many people are in your (and your spouse's) <u>household</u>? **See page 7.**

87. How many in question 86 will be <u>college students</u> between July 1, 2000, and June 30, 2001? **Do not include your parents. See page 7.**

Step Six: Please tell us which schools should receive your information.

For each school (up to six), please provide the federal school code and your housing plans (**enter "1" for on campus, "2" for off campus, and "3" for with parents**). Look for the federal school codes on the Internet at **http://www.ed.gov/studentaid**, at your college financial aid office, at your public library, or by asking your high school guidance counselor. If you cannot get the federal school code, write in the complete name, address, city, and state of the college.

Federal school code *OR* Name of college	College street address and city	State	Housing Plans
FIRST SCHOOL CODE **88.**			**89.**
SECOND SCHOOL CODE **90.**			**91.**
THIRD SCHOOL CODE **92.**			**93.**
FOURTH SCHOOL CODE **94.**			**95.**
FIFTH SCHOOL CODE **96.**			**97.**
SIXTH SCHOOL CODE **98.**			**99.**

Step Seven: Please read, sign, and date.

By signing this application, you agree, if asked, to provide information that will verify the accuracy of your completed form. This information may include a copy of your U.S. or state income tax form. Also, you certify that you (1) will use federal and/or state student financial aid only to pay the cost of attending an institution of higher education, (2) are not in default on a federal student loan or have made satisfactory arrangements to repay it, (3) do not owe money back on a federal student grant or have made satisfactory arrangements to repay it, (4) will notify your school if you default on a federal student loan, and (5) understand that **the Secretary of Education has the authority to verify income reported on this application with the Internal Revenue Service.** If you purposely give false or misleading information, you may be fined $10,000, sent to prison, or both.

100. Date this form was completed.

MONTH / DAY / **2000** ○ or **2001** ○

101. Student signature   (Sign in box)

¹ FOR INFORMATION ONLY

Parent signature (one parent whose information is provided in Step Four.)   (Sign in box)

² DO NOT SUBMIT

If this form was filled out by someone other than you, your spouse, or your parent(s), that person must complete this part.

Preparer's
Name and Firm _____

Address _____

SCHOOL USE ONLY
D/O ○ ¹   Federal School Code
FAA SIGNATURE
¹

102. Social Security #   ☐☐☐ – ☐☐ – ☐☐☐☐
OR
103. Employer ID #   ☐☐ – ☐☐☐☐☐☐☐

104. Signature
and Date ¹ _____

MDE USE ONLY
Special Handle   ☐ – ☐☐☐☐☐☐

CSS/FINANCIAL AID

 **2000-2001**

NOTE: SAMPLE ONLY

Application

FOR INFORMATION ONLY. DO NOT SUBMIT

Section A - Student's Information

1. How many people are in the student's (and spouse's) household? <u>Always include the student (and spouse).</u> List their names and give information about them in Section M. See instructions.

2. Of the number in 1, how many will be college students between July 1, 2000 and June 30, 2001? Include yourself.

3. What is the student's state of legal residence?

4. What is the student's citizenship status?

   a. 1 ○ U.S. citizen (Skip to Question 5.)
      2 ○ Eligible non-citizen - see instructions. (Skip to Question 5.)
      3 ○ Neither of the above (Answer 'b' and 'c' below.)

   b. Country of citizenship?

   c. Visa classification?
      1 ○ F1   2 ○ F2   3 ○ J1   4 ○ J2   5 ○ G   6 ○ Other

Section B - Student's 1999 Income & Benefits

If married, include spouse's information in Sections B, C, D, and E.

5. The following 1999 U.S. Income tax return figures are (Fill in only one oval.)
   1 ○ estimated. Will file IRS Form 1040EZ, 1040A, or 1040TEL. Go to 6.
   2 ○ estimated. Will file IRS Form 1040. Go to 6.
   3 ○ from a completed IRS Form 1040EZ, 1040A, or 1040TEL. Go to 6.
   4 ○ from a completed IRS Form 1040. Go to 6.
   5 ○ a tax return will not be filed. Skip to 10.

Tax Filers Only

6. 1999 total number of exemptions (IRS Form 1040, line 6d or 1040A, line 6d or 1040EZ - see instructions.)

7. 1999 Adjusted Gross Income from IRS Form 1040, line 33 or 1040A, line 18 or 1040EZ, line 4 $ _____ .00

8. a. 1999 U.S. income tax paid (IRS Form 1040, line 49 or 1040A, line 32 or 1040EZ, line 10) $ _____ .00

   b. 1999 Education Credits-Hope and Lifetime Learning (IRS Form 1040, line 44 or 1040A, line 29) $ _____ .00

9. 1999 Itemized deductions (IRS Form 1040, Schedule A, line 28. Write in "0" if deductions were not itemized.) $ _____ .00

10. 1999 income earned from work by student (See instructions.) $ _____ .00

11. 1999 income earned from work by student's spouse $ _____ .00

12. 1999 dividend and interest income $ _____ .00

13. 1999 untaxed income and benefits (Give total amount for year.)

    a. Social security benefits (See instructions.) $ _____ .00

    b. AFDC/ADC or TANF (See instructions.) $ _____ .00

    c. Child support received for all children $ _____ .00

    d. Earned Income Credit (IRS Form 1040, line 59a or 1040A, line 37a or 1040EZ, line 8a) $ _____ .00

    e. Other - write total from instruction worksheet, page 4. $ _____ .00

14. 1999 earnings from Federal Work-Study or other need-based work programs plus any grant and scholarship aid required to be reported on your U.S. income tax return $ _____ .00

Section C - Student's Assets

Include trust accounts only in Section D.

15. Cash, savings, and checking accounts $ _____ .00

16. Total value of IRA, Keogh, 401k, 403b, etc. accounts as of December 31, 1999. $ _____ .00

17. Investments (Including Uniform Gifts to Minors. See instructions.)
    What is it worth today? $ _____ .00
    What is owed on it? $ _____ .00

18. Home (Renters write in "0".)
    $ _____ .00 $ _____ .00

19. Other real estate
    $ _____ .00 $ _____ .00

20. Business and farm
    $ _____ .00 $ _____ .00

21. If a farm is included in 20, is the student living on the farm?   Yes ○ 1   No ○ 2

22. If student owns home, give
    a. year purchased _____
    b. purchase price $ _____ .00

Section D - Student's Trust Information

23. a. Total value of all trust(s) $ _____ .00

    b. Is any income or part of the principal currently available?
       Yes ○ 1   No ○ 2

    c. Who established the trust(s)?
       1 ○ Student's parents   2 ○ Other

Section E - Student's 1999 Expenses

24. 1999 child support paid because of divorce or separation $ _____ .00

25. 1999 medical and dental expenses not covered by insurance (See instructions.) $ _____ .00

Section F - Student's Expected Summer /School-Year Resources for 2000-2001

	Amount per month	Number of months
26. Student's veterans benefits (July 1, 2000 - June 30, 2001.)	$ .00	☐☐

27. Student's (and spouse's) resources
(Don't enter monthly amounts.)

	Summer 2000 (3 months)	School Year 2000-2001 (9 months)
a. Student's wages, salaries, tips, etc.	$ .00	$ .00
b. Spouse's wages, salaries, tips, etc.	$ .00	$ .00
c. Other taxable income	$ .00 ·	$ .00
d. Untaxed income and benefits	$ .00	$ .00
e. Grants, scholarships, fellowships, etc. from sources other than the colleges or universities to which the student is applying (List sources in Section P.)		$ .00
f. Tuition benefits from the parents' and/or the student's or spouse's employer		$ .00
g. Amount the student's parent(s) think they will be able to pay for the student's 2000-2001 college expenses		$ .00
h. Amounts expected from other relatives, spouse's parents, and all other sources (List sources in Section P.)		$ .00

Section G - Parents' Household Information - See page 5 of the instruction booklet.

28. How many people are in your parents' household? Always include the student and parents. List their names and give information about them in Section M. See instructions. ☐☐

29. Of the number in 28, how many will be college students between July 1, 2000 and June 30, 2001. Include the student. ☐

30. How many parents will be in college at least half-time in 2000-2001? (Fill in only one oval.)

₁ ◯ Neither parent   ₂ ◯ One parent   ₃ ◯ Both parents

31. What is the current marital status of your parents? (Fill in only one oval.)

₁ ◯ single   ₃ ◯ separated   ₅ ◯ widowed

₂ ◯ married   ₄ ◯ divorced

32. What is your parents' state of legal residence? ☐☐

Section H - Parents' Expenses

		1999	Expected 2000
33. Child support paid because of divorce or separation	**33.**	$ .00	$ .00
34. Repayment of parents' educational loans (See instructions.)	**34.**	$ .00	$ .00
35. Medical and dental expenses not covered by insurance (See instructions.)	**35.**	$ .00	$ .00
36. Total elementary, junior high school, and high school tuition paid for dependent children			
a. Amount paid (Don't include tuition paid for the student.)	**36.**	$ .00	$ .00
b. For how many dependent children? (Don't include the student.)		☐	☐

Section I - Parents' Assets - If parents own all or part of a business or farm, write in its name and the percent of ownership in Section P.

	What is it worth today?	What is owed on it?
37. Cash, savings, and checking accounts	$ .00	**41.** Business $ .00 $ .00
38. Total value of assets held in the names of the student's brothers and sisters who are under age 19 and not college students	$ .00	**42.** a. Farm $ .00 $ .00

42. b. Does family live on the farm?

Yes ◯₁ No ◯₂

	What is it worth today?	What is owed on it?
39. Investments	$ .00	$ .00
40. a. Home (Renters write in "0". Skip to 40d.)	$ .00	$ .00
b. Year purchased ☐☐☐☐	c. Purchase price	$ .00

43. a. Other real estate $ .00 $ 00

b. Year purchased ☐☐☐☐   c. Purchase price $ 00

40. d. Monthly home mortgage or rental payment (If none, explain in Section P.) $ .00

Section J - Parents' 1998 Income & Benefits

44. **1998 Adjusted Gross Income** (IRS Form 1040, line 33 or 1040A, line 18 or 1040EZ, line 4) $ _____.00

45. **1998 U.S. income tax paid** (IRS Form 1040, line 49, 1040A, line 32 or 1040EZ, line 10) $ _____.00

46. **1998 Itemized deductions** (IRS Form 1040, Schedule A, line 28. Write "0" if deductions were not itemized.) $ _____.00

47. **1998 untaxed income and benefits** (Include the same types of income & benefits that are listed in 55 a-k.) $ _____.00

Section K - Parents' 1999 Income & Benefits

48. **The following 1999 U.S. income tax return figures are** (Fill in only one oval.)

| ₁ ○ estimated. Will file IRS Form 1040EZ, 1040A, or 1040TEL. Go to 49. | ₂ ○ estimated. Will file IRS Form 1040. Go to 49. | ₃ ○ from a completed IRS Form 1040EZ, 1040A, or 1040TEL. Go to 49. | ₄ ○ from a completed IRS Form 1040. Go to 49. | ₅ ○ a tax return will not be filed. Skip to 53. |

Tax Filers Only

49. **1999 total number of exemptions** (IRS Form 1040, line 6d or 1040A, line 6d or 1040EZ - see instructions)   **49.** ⌐⌐

50. **1999 Adjusted Gross Income** (IRS Form 1040, line 33 or 1040A, line 18 or 1040EZ, line 4)   **50.** $ _____.00

   Breakdown of income in 50

   a. Wages, salaries, tips (IRS Form 1040, line 7 or 1040A, line 7 or 1040EZ, line 1)   **50.** **a.** $ _____.00

   b. Interest income (IRS Form 1040, line 8a or 1040A, line 8a or 1040EZ, line 2)   **b.** $ _____.00

   c. Dividend income (IRS Form 1040, line 9 or 1040A, line 9)   **c.** $ _____.00

   d. Net income (or loss) from business, farm, rents, royalties, partnerships, estates, trusts, etc. (IRS Form 1040, lines 12, 17, and 18). If a loss, enter the amount in (parentheses).   **d.** $ _____.00

   e. Other taxable income such as alimony received, capital gains (or losses), pensions, annuities, etc. (IRS Form 1040, lines 10, 11, 13, 14, 15b, 16b, 19, 20b and 21 or 1040A, lines 10b, 11b, 12, and 13b or 1040EZ, line 3)   **e.** $ _____.00

   f. Adjustments to income (IRS Form 1040, line 32 or 1040A, line 17- see instructions.)   **f.** $ _____.00

51. **a. 1999 U.S. income tax paid** (IRS Form 1040, line 49, 1040A, line 32 or 1040EZ, line 10)   **51. a.** $ _____.00

   b. 1999 Education Credits-Hope and Lifetime Learning (IRS Form 1040, line 44 or 1040A, line 29)   **b.** $ _____.00

52. **1999 itemized deductions** (IRS Form 1040, Schedule A, line 28. Write in "0" if deductions were not itemized.)   **52.** $ _____.00

53. **1999 income earned from work by father/stepfather**   **53.** $ _____.00

54. **1999 income earned from work by mother/stepmother**   **54.** $ _____.00

55. **1999 untaxed income and benefits** (Give total amount for the year. Do not give monthly amounts.)

   a. Social security benefits received   **55. a.** $ _____.00

   b. AFDC/ADC or TANF (See instructions.)   **b.** $ _____.00

   c. Child support received for all children   **c.** $ _____.00

   d. Deductible IRA and/or Keogh payments (See instructions.)   **d.** $ _____.00

   e. Payments to tax-deferred pension and savings plans (See instructions.)   **e.** $ _____.00

   f. Amounts withheld from wages for dependent care and medical spending accounts   **f.** $ _____.00

   g. Earned Income Credit (IRS Form 1040, line 59a or 1040A, line 37a or 1040EZ, line 8a)   **g.** $ _____.00

   h. Housing, food and other living allowances (See instructions.)   **h.** $ _____.00

   i. Tax-exempt interest income (IRS Form 1040, line 8b or 1040A, line 8b)   **i.** $ _____.00

   j. Foreign income exclusion (IRS Form 2555, line 43 or Form 2555EZ, line 18)   **j.** $ _____.00

   k. Other - write in the total from the worksheet in the instructions, page 7.   **k.** $ _____.00

WRITE ONLY IN THE ANSWER SPACES. DO NOT WRITE ANYWHERE ELSE.

Section L - Parents' 2000 Expected Income & Benefits
If the expected total income and benefits will differ from the 1999 total income by $3,000 or more, explain in Section P.

56. **2000 income earned from work by father** $ _____.00

58. **2000 other taxable income** $ _____.00

57. **2000 income earned from work by mother** $ _____.00

59. **2000 untaxed income and benefits** (See 55a-k.) $ _____.00

Section M - Family Member Listing - Give information for all family members entered in question 1 or 28. List up to seven family members in addition to the student. If there are more than seven, list first those who will be in school or college at least half-time. List the others in Section P. Leave shaded sections blank.

60.

	Full name of family member	Use codes from below.	Age (Required)	Claimed by parents as tax exemption in 1999? Yes?	No?	1999-2000 school year Name of school or college	Year in school	Scholarships and grants	Parents' contri-bution	2000-2001 school year Attend college at least one term full-time	half-time	College or university Type	Name
1	You - the student applicant			○	○			$	$				
2				○	○			$	$	1 ○	2 ○		
3				○	○			$	$	1 ○	2 ○		
4				○	○			$	$	1 ○	2 ○		
5				○	○			$	$	1 ○	2 ○		
6				○	○			$	$	1 ○	2 ○		
7				○	○			$	$	1 ○	2 ○		
8				○	○			$	$	1 ○	2 ○		

Write in the correct code from the right.   1 – Student's parent, 2 – Student's stepparent, 3 – Student's brother or sister, 4 – Student's husband or wife, 5 – Student's son or daughter, 6 – Student's grandparent, 7 – Student's stepbrother or stepsister, 8 – Other   Write in the correct code from the instructions on page 8.

Section N - Parents' Information (to be answered by the parent(s) completing this form)

61. Fill in one: ○ Father ○ Stepfather ○ Legal guardian ○ Other (Explain in P.)

62. Fill in one: ○ Mother ○ Stepmother ○ Legal guardian ○ Other (Explain in P.)

a. Name _____ Age ☐☐

b. Fill in if: ○ Self-employed ○ Unemployed - Date: _____

c. Occupation _____

d. Employer _____ No. years _____

e. Work telephone ☐☐☐ – ☐☐☐ – ☐☐☐☐

f. Retirement plans: ○ Social security ○ Union/employer ○ Civil service/state ○ IRA/Keogh/tax-deferred ○ Military ○ Other

a. Name _____ Age ☐☐

b. Fill in if: ○ Self-employed ○ Unemployed - Date: _____

c. Occupation _____

d. Employer _____ No. years _____

e. Work telephone ☐☐☐ – ☐☐☐ – ☐☐☐☐

f. Retirement plans: ○ Social security ○ Union/employer ○ Civil service/state ○ IRA/Keogh/tax-deferred ○ Military ○ Other

Section O - Information About Noncustodial Parent (to be answered by the parent who completes this form if the student's biological or adoptive parents are divorced, separated, or were never married to each other)

63.

a. Noncustodial parent's name: _____
   Home address _____
   _____
   Occupation/Employer _____

b. Year of separation ☐☐☐☐ Year of divorce ☐☐☐☐

c. According to court order, when will support for the student end? ☐☐ Month ☐☐☐☐ Year

d. Who last claimed the student as a tax exemption? _____ Year? ☐☐☐☐

e. How much does the noncustodial parent plan to contribute to the student's education for the 2000-2001 school year? (Do not include this amount in 27g.) $_____ .00

f. Is there an agreement specifying this contribution for the student's education? Yes ○ No ○

Section P - Explanations/Special Circumstances
Explain any unusual expenses such as high medical or dental expenses, educational and other debts, child care, elder care, or special circumstances. Also, give information for any outside scholarships you have been awarded. If more space is needed, use sheets of paper and send them directly to your schools and programs. (please print)

Certification:
All the information on this form is true and complete to the best of my knowledge. If asked, I agree to give proof of the information that I have given on this form. I realize that this proof may include a copy of my U.S., state, or local income tax returns. I certify that all information is correct at the time, and that I will send timely notice to my schools/programs of any significant change in family income or assets, financial situation, college plans of other children, or the receipt of other scholarships or grants.

1. Student's signature _____
2. Student's spouse's signature _____

3. Father's (stepfather's) signature _____
4. Mother's (stepmother's) signature _____

MAIL COMPLETED APPLICATION TO: COLLEGE SCHOLARSHIP SERVICE
P.O. BOX 4004
MOUNT VERNON, IL 62864-8604

Date completed: ☐☐ Month ☐☐ Day
1 ○ 1999
2 ○ 2000

CSS Use Only	
	W
	B
	G
	S

EXPECTED FAMILY CONTRIBUTION: SAMPLE ANALYSES

For planning and budgeting purposes, it is important for students and parents to have an estimate of their expected family contribution (EFC) as early as possible. As noted in chapter 2, the EFC is the key to all financial aid, whether the student plans to attend a community college, a four-year public institution, or a four-year private college.

The EFC estimates on the following pages illustrate analyses of various families incomes and assets as determined by the students' FAFSA (Free Application for Federal Student Aid). All names and figures are fictitious, although the expected family contribution is based on the formula used by the U.S. Department of Education, which administers the FAFSA. Please note that *home equity,* shown under line 14, "Cash & Bank Accounts," is not calculated as part of the "Parents' Contribution From Assets." For a free EFC estimate on-line, log on to either of the following web addresses:

- www.collegeboard.org/finaid/fastud/html/efc.htm
- www.finaid.org/calculators/finaidestimate.phtml

INDEPENDENT STATUS

Of course, different criteria apply for students who are classified as *independent,* where the parents' income and assets are not considered. To be classified as an *independent,* students must be able to meet one of the following requirements:

1. Be twenty-four years of age by December 31 of the year preceding application

2. Be an orphan or ward of the court

3. Be a veteran of the Armed Services

4. Be a professional or graduate student

5. Be married with or without dependents

6. Have dependents other than a spouse

7. Be judged independent by the college financial aid administrator

Family Contribution For: JASON
Student Name: JASON
Dependent Students

CONTRIBUTION FROM PARENTS' INCOME
1. Parents' Adjusted Gross Income $ 51,380
2. Parents' Untaxed Social Security Benefits $ 0
3. Parents' Aid to Families with Dependent Children Benefit $ 0
4. Parents' Other Non-Taxable Income $ 0
5. Deductible IRA, 401K, & KEOGH Payments $ 0
6. Total Income $ 51,380
7. U.S. Income Tax Paid $ 4,965
8. State Tax Allowance (IA - Iowa) $ 3,597
9. Social Security Taxes Paid $ 3,931
10. Income Protection Allowance
    based on 4 Family Members & 2 Student(s) in College $ 16,060
11. Employment Expense Allowance $ 2,700
12. Total Allowances $ 31,252
13. Parents' Available Income $ 20,128

PARENTS' CONTRIBUTION FROM ASSETS
14. Cash & Bank Accounts $ 3,200
    Home Equity $ 0
15. Other Real Estate, Investments, Stocks, Bonds, Trusts, Etc. $ 40,000
16. Adjusted Business and/or Commercial Farm Net Worth $ 0
17. Total Assets $ 43,200
18. Asset Protection Allowance
    Two-Parent, Two-Income Family, Older Parent Age = 49 $ 44,500
19. Discretionary Net Worth $ 0
20. CONTRIBUTION FROM ASSETS $ 0

PARENTAL CONTRIBUTION
21. Adjusted Available Income $ 20,128
22. PARENT CONTRIBUTION $ 5,303
23. Number in College Adjustment. (2 Student(s))
    Contribution for Each Student $ 2,652

STUDENT'S CONTRIBUTION FROM INCOME
24. JASON's Adjusted Gross Income $ 1,200
25. Untaxed Social Security Benefits student will receive
    from 1996/1997 year $ 0
26. Other Untaxed Income and Benefits. Include IRA payments $ 0
27. Total Income for JASON $ 1,200
28. JASON's U.S. Income Taxes $ 0
29. JASON's State Tax Allowance (IA - Iowa) $ 60
30. JASON's Social Security Taxes $ 92
31. Income Protection Allowance $ 1,750
32. Total Student's Allowance for JASON $ 1,902
33. JASON's Available Income $ 0
34. STUDENT'S CONTRIBUTION FROM INCOME (JASON) $ 0

STUDENT'S CONTRIBUTION FROM ASSETS
35. ALL of JASON's Assets: Savings,Trusts,Real Estate $ 900
36. STUDENT'S CONTRIBUTION FROM ASSETS $ 315

EXPECTED FAMILY CONTRIBUTION
37. Family Contribution for 2 Students in College (JASON) $ 2,967

EFC calculates 2,967 for each of two students.

INDEPENDENT STUDENTS WITH DEPENDENTS

Family Contribution For: JEROME
Student Name: JEROME

CONTRIBUTION FROM INCOME
```
 1. Student's (& Spouse's) Adjusted Gross Income            $    21,012
 2. Student's (& Spouse's) Social Security Benefits         $         0
 3. Student's (& Spouse's) Aid to Families                  $         0
 4. Student's (& Spouse's) Other Non-Taxable Income         $         0
 5. Student (& Spouse's) Deductible IRA, 401k & KEOGH Payments $      0
 6. Total Income                                            $    21,012
 7. U.S. Income Tax Paid                                    $     1,767
 8. State Tax Allowance ( MI - Michigan)                    $     1,496
 9. Social Security Taxes Paid                              $     1,431
10. Income Protection Allowance
    based on  3 Family Members &  1 Student(s) in College   $    14,630
11. Employment Expense Allowance                            $         0
12. Total Allowances                                        $    19,324
13. Available Income                                        $     1,688
```

CONTRIBUTION FROM ASSETS
```
14. Cash & Bank Accounts                                    $       100
    Home Equity                                             $         0
15. Other Real Estate, Investments, Stocks, Bonds, Trusts, Etc. $ 2,200
16. Adjusted Business and/or Commercial Farm Net Worth      $         0
17. Total Assets                                            $     2,300
18. Asset Protection Allowance: Married
    One-Income Family, Student Age =  22                    $         0
19. Discretionary Net Worth                                 $     2,300
20. CONTRIBUTION FROM ASSETS                                $       276
21. Adjusted Available Income                               $     1,964
22. TOTAL CONTRIBUTION                                      $       432

23. Number in College Adjustment. ( 1 Student(s))
    Contribution for Each Student                           $       432
```

Pell & SEOG likely based upon low EFC.

INDEPENDENT STUDENTS WITHOUT DEPENDENTS

Family Contribution For: REGGIE
Student Name: REGGIE

CONTRIBUTION FROM INCOME

1. Student's (& Spouse's) Adjusted Gross Income	$	15,010
2. Student's (& Spouse's) Social Security Benefits	$	0
3. Student's (& Spouse's) Aid to Families	$	0
4. Student's (& Spouse's) Other Non-Taxable Income	$	0
5. Student (& Spouse's) Deductible IRA, 401k & KEOGH Payments	$	0
6. Total Income	$	15,010
7. U.S. Income Tax Paid	$	1,368
8. State Tax Allowance (IL - Illinois)	$	729
9. Social Security Taxes Paid	$	929
10. Income Protection Allowance based on 2 Family Members & 1 Student(s) in College	$	6,000
11. Employment Expense Allowance	$	0
12. Total Allowances	$	9,026
13. Available Income	$	5,984
14. Contribution from Income	$	2,992

CONTRIBUTION FROM ASSETS

15. Cash & Bank Accounts	$	220
Home Equity	$	0
16. Other Real Estate, Investments, Stocks, Bonds, Trusts, Etc.	$	0
17. Adjusted Business and/or Commercial Farm Net Worth	$	0
18. Total Assets	$	220
19. Asset Protection Allowance: Married - One Enrolled H/T+ One-Income Family, Student Age = 19	$	0
20. Discretionary Net Worth	$	220
21. CONTRIBUTION FROM ASSETS	$	77
22. Adjusted Available Income	$	3,069
23. TOTAL CONTRIBUTION	$	3,069
24. Number in College Adjustment. (1 Student(s)) Contribution for Each Student	$	3,069

Family Contribution For: ROBIN
Student Name: ROBIN
Dependent Students

CONTRIBUTION FROM PARENTS' INCOME
1. Parents' Adjusted Gross Income $ 29,897
2. Parents' Untaxed Social Security Benefits $ 0
3. Parents' Aid to Families with Dependent Children Benefit $ 0
4. Parents' Other Non-Taxable Income $ 300
5. Deductible IRA, 401K, & KEOGH Payments $ 0
6. Total Income $ 30,197
7. U.S. Income Tax Paid $ 2,100
8. State Tax Allowance (PA - Pennsylvania) $ 1,812
9. Social Security Taxes Paid $ 2,287
10. Income Protection Allowance
    based on 4 Family Members & 1 Student(s) in College $ 18,070
11. Employment Expense Allowance $ 2,700
12. Total Allowances $ 26,969
13. Parents' Available Income $ 3,228

PARENTS' CONTRIBUTION FROM ASSETS
14. Cash & Bank Accounts $ 225
    Home Equity $ 0
15. Other Real Estate, Investments, Stocks, Bonds, Trusts, Etc. $ 0
16. Adjusted Business and/or Commercial Farm Net Worth $ 0
17. Total Assets $ 225
18. Asset Protection Allowance
    One-Parent, One-Income Family, Older Parent Age = 44 $ 27,100
19. Discretionary Net Worth $ 0
20. CONTRIBUTION FROM ASSETS $ 0

PARENTAL CONTRIBUTION
21. Adjusted Available Income $ 3,228
22. PARENT CONTRIBUTION $ 710
23. Number in College Adjustment. (1 Student(s))
    Contribution for Each Student $ 710

STUDENT'S CONTRIBUTION FROM INCOME
24. ROBIN's Adjusted Gross Income $ 2,100
25. Untaxed Social Security Benefits student will receive
    from 1996/1997 year $ 0
26. Other Untaxed Income and Benefits. Include IRA payments $ 0
27. Total Income for ROBIN $ 2,100
28. ROBIN's U.S. Income Taxes $ 0
29. ROBIN's State Tax Allowance (PA - Pennsylvania) $ 63
30. ROBIN's Social Security Taxes $ 161
31. Income Protection Allowance $ 1,750
32. Total Student's Allowance for ROBIN $ 1,974
33. ROBIN's Available Income $ 126
34. STUDENT'S CONTRIBUTION FROM INCOME (ROBIN) $ 63

STUDENT'S CONTRIBUTION FROM ASSETS
35. ALL of ROBIN's Assets: Savings,Trusts,Real Estate $ 875
36. STUDENT'S CONTRIBUTION FROM ASSETS $ 306

EXPECTED FAMILY CONTRIBUTION
37. Family Contribution for 1 Students in College (ROBIN) $ 1,080

Based upon EFC, Robin may qualify for Pell & SEOG.

Family Contribution For: STEPHANIE
Student Name: STEPHANIE
Dependent Students

CONTRIBUTION FROM PARENTS' INCOME
1. Parents' Adjusted Gross Income $ 38,000
2. Parents' Untaxed Social Security Benefits $ 0
3. Parents' Aid to Families with Dependent Children Benefit $ 0
4. Parents' Other Non-Taxable Income $ 0
5. Deductible IRA, 401K, & KEOGH Payments $ 2,500
6. Total Income $ 40,500
7. U.S. Income Tax Paid $ 4,463
8. State Tax Allowance (CA - California) $ 3,086
9. Social Security Taxes Paid $ 3
10. Income Protection Allowance
    based on 5 Family Members & 1 Student(s) in College $ 21,320
11. Employment Expense Allowance $ 2,700
12. Total Allowances $ 31,572
13. Parents' Available Income $ 8,928

PARENTS' CONTRIBUTION FROM ASSETS
14. Cash & Bank Accounts $ 2,450
    Home Equity $ 0
15. Other Real Estate, Investments, Stocks, Bonds, Trusts, Etc. $ 41,700
16. Adjusted Business and/or Commercial Farm Net Worth $ 0
17. Total Assets $ 44,150
18. Asset Protection Allowance
    Two-Parent, Two-Income Family, Older Parent Age = 52 $ 48,300
19. Discretionary Net Worth $ 0
20. CONTRIBUTION FROM ASSETS $ 0

PARENTAL CONTRIBUTION
21. Adjusted Available Income $ 8,928
22. PARENT CONTRIBUTION $ 1,964
23. Number in College Adjustment. (1 Student(s))
    Contribution for Each Student $ 1,964

STUDENT'S CONTRIBUTION FROM INCOME
24. STEPHANIE's Adjusted Gross Income $ 1,600
25. Untaxed Social Security Benefits student will receive
    from 1996/1997 year $ 0
26. Other Untaxed Income and Benefits. Include IRA payments $ 0
27. Total Income for STEPHANIE $ 1,600
28. STEPHANIE's U.S. Income Taxes $ 0
29. STEPHANIE's State Tax Allowance (CA - California) $ 80
30. STEPHANIE's Social Security Taxes $ 122
31. Income Protection Allowance $ 1,750
32. Total Student's Allowance for STEPHANIE $ 1,952
33. STEPHANIE's Available Income $ 0
34. STUDENT'S CONTRIBUTION FROM INCOME (STEPHANIE) $ 0

STUDENT'S CONTRIBUTION FROM ASSETS
35. ALL of STEPHANIE's Assets: Savings,Trusts,Real Estate $ 600
36. STUDENT'S CONTRIBUTION FROM ASSETS $ 210

EXPECTED FAMILY CONTRIBUTION
37. Family Contribution for 1 Students in College (STEPHANIE) $ 2,174

Based upon EFC, Stephanie may qualify for small Pell

STATE GRANTS

State agencies administer the federally funded Leveraging Educational Assistance Partnership (LEAP). Below is a list of the agencies students may contact for more information. (Check the phone directory for any address, area code, or phone number changes.)

ALABAMA
Higher Education Commission
3465 Norman Bridge Rd.
Montgomery, AL 36105
(334) 281-1998

ALASKA
Education Commission
3030 Vintage Blvd.
Juneau, AK 99801
(907) 465-2967

ARIZONA
Education Commission
2020 North Central
Phoenix, AZ 85004
(602) 229-2531

ARKANSAS
Department of Education
114 East Capitol Street
Little Rock, AR 72201
(501) 324-9300

CALIFORNIA
Student Aid Commission
P.O. Box 419026
Rancho Cordova, CA 95670
(916) 526-7590

COLORADO
Education Commission
1300 Broadway, 2nd Floor
Denver, CO 80203
(303) 866-2723

CONNECTICUT
Department of Higher Education
61 Woodland Street
Hartford, CT 06105
(203) 566-3910

DELAWARE
Higher Education Commission
820 North French Street
Wilmington, DE 19801
(302) 577-3240

DISTRICT OF COLUMBIA
Education Assistance
2100 M.L. King Jr. Avenue
Washington, DC 20020
(202) 727-3685

FLORIDA
Student Financial Assistance
325 W. Gaines Street
Tallahassee, FL 32399
(904) 487-0649

GEORGIA
Student Finance Commission
2082 East Exchange Place
Tucker, GA 30084
(770) 414-3000

HAWAII
Postsecondary Education Commission
2444 Dole Street, Room 202
Honolulu, HI 96822
(808) 956-8213

IDAHO
Idaho Board of Education
P.O. Box 83720
Boise, ID 83720
(208) 334-2270

ILLINOIS
Assistance Commission
1755 Lake Cook Road
Deerfield, IL 60015
(847) 948-8500

INDIANA
Assistance Commission
150 West Market Street,
Indianapolis, IN 46204
(317) 232-2350

IOWA
Student Aid Commission
914 Grand Avenue
Des Moines, IA 50309
(800) 383-4222

KANSAS
Kansas Board of Regents
700 SW Harrison
Topeka, KS 66603
(913) 296-3517

KENTUCKY
Higher Education Assistance
1050 US 127 South
Frankfort, KY 40601
(800) 928-8926

LOUISIANA
Assistance Commission
P.O. Box 91202
Baton Rouge, LA 70821
(800) 259-5626

MAINE
Finance Authority of Maine
P.O. Box 949
Augusta, ME 04333
(207) 287-3263

MARYLAND
Higher Education Commission
16 Francis Street
Annapolis, MD 21401
(410) 974-2971

MASSACHUSETTS
Higher Education Board
330 Stuart Street
Boston, MA 02116
(617) 727-9420

MICHIGAN
Higher Education Authority
P.O. Box 30462
Lansing, MI 48909
(517) 373-3394

MINNESOTA
Higher Education Services
550 Cedar Street, Suite 400
St. Paul, MN 55101
(800) 657-3866

MISSISSIPPI
Financial Assistance Board
3825 Ridgewood Road
Jackson, MS 39211
(601) 982-6663

MISSOURI
Higher Education Board
3515 Amazonas Drive
Jefferson City, MO 65109
(314) 751-2361

MONTANA
Montana University System
2500 Broadway
Helena, MT 59620
(406) 444-6570

NEBRASKA
Education Commission
P.O. Box 95005
Lincoln, NE 68509
(402) 471-5915

NEVADA
Department of Education
400 West King Street
Carson City, NV 89710
(702) 687-3100

NEW HAMPSHIRE
Education Commission
Two Industrial Park Drive
Concord, NH 03301
(603) 271-2555

NEW JERSEY
Office of Student Assistance
4 Quakerbridge Plaza
Trenton, NJ 08625
(800) 792-8670

NEW MEXICO
Education Commission
1068 Cerrillos Road
Santa Fe, NM 87501
(505) 827-7383

NEW YORK
Higher Education Service
One Commerce Plaza
Albany, NY 12255
(518) 474-5642

NORTH CAROLINA
State Education Assistance
P.O. Box 2688
Chapel Hill, NC 27515
(919) 821-4771

NORTH DAKOTA
Student Financial Assistance
600 East Boulevard Avenue
Bismarck, ND 58505
(701) 224-4114

OHIO
Board of Regents
P.O. Box 182452
Columbus, OH 43218
(888) 833-1133

OKLAHOMA
State Regents for Higher Education
P.O. Box 3000
Oklahoma City, OK 73101
(405) 858-4300

OREGON
State Scholarship Commission
1500 Valley River Dr., Suite 100
Eugene, OR 97401
(503) 687-7400

PENNSYLVANIA
Higher Education Assistance
1200 North Seventh Street
Harrisburg, PA 17102
(800) 692-7435

RHODE ISLAND
Higher Education Assistance
560 Jefferson Boulevard
Warwick, RI 02886
(800) 922-9855

SOUTH CAROLINA
Higher Education
P.O. Box 12159
Columbia, SC 29211
(803) 734-1200

SOUTH DAKOTA
Department of Education
700 Governors Drive
Pierre, SD 57501
(605) 773-3134

TENNESSEE
Student Assistance
404 James Robertson Parkway
Nashville, TN 37243
(615) 741-3605

TEXAS
Higher Education Board
Box 12788 Capitol Station
Austin, TX 78711
(800) 242-3062

UTAH
Utah State Board of Regents
3 Triad Center, Suite 550
Salt Lake City, UT 84180
(801) 321-7205

VERMONT
Student Assistance
P.O. Box 2000
Winooski, VT 05404
(800) 642-3177

VIRGINIA
Higher Education Council
101 North Fourteenth Street
Richmond, VA 23219
(804) 786-1690

WASHINGTON
Higher Education Board
Box 43430
Olympia, WA 98504
(206) 753-7850

WEST VIRGINIA
Department of Education
1900 Washington Street
Charleston, WV 25305
(304) 588-2691

WISCONSIN
Higher Education Board
P.O. Box 7885
Madison, WI 53707
(608) 267-2206

WYOMING
Department of Education
2300 Capitol Avenue
Cheyenne, WY 82002
(307) 777-6265

GUAM
University of Guam
303 University Drive
Mangiloa, Guam 96923
(671) 734-4469

PUERTO RICO
Council on Higher Education
Box 23305 - UPR Station
Rio Piedras, Puerto Rico 00931
(787) 724-7100

VIRGIN ISLANDS
Joint Boards of Education
P.O. Box 11900
St. Thomas, Virgin Islands 00801
(809) 774-4546

INTERNET CONNECTIONS AND SCHOLARSHIP SEARCHES

The following addresses may be helpful for students who wish to visit different campuses on-line, plan to file their college application via their home computer, or seek student financial aid:

- All Campus at http://www.allcampus.com
- Apply at http://www.review.com/
- College Board at http://collegeboard.org
- Peterson's at http://www.petersons.com
- College Link at http://www.collegelink.com
- College View at http://www.collegeview.com
- College Net at http://www.collegenet.com
- Campus Tours at http://www.campustours.com
- Embark*Com at http://www.embark.com
- College Town at http://www.collegetownusa.com
- U.S. News at http://www.usnews.com/usnews/edu/
- U.S. Students at http://www.nyu.edu/ssgs/ssgsplan.html

For additional insight, order *Internet Guide for College-Bound Students* from the College Board at 800-323-7155. The cost is $14.95 plus $4.00 shipping and handling.

Helpful scholarship searches can be found on the Internet *free* of charge. They are:

1. Mark Kantrowitz at http://www.finaid.org
2. College Board at http://collegeboard.org
3. fastWeb at http://www.fastweb.com
4. FreSch! at http://www.freschinfo.com
5. CASHE at http://scholarships.salliemae.com

FreSch! Information Services offers an extensive database which can be searched for free at www.freschinfo.com. The search service will match the student with all the possible sources that apply based on a student's completed biographical survey of backgrounds, skills, and interests. For students without Internet access, FreSch! also offers an off-line search for $5.00. If no scholarship matches are found, the student will receive a full refund.

According to FreSch!, there is no upper age limit for most scholarships in the database. "The search can be as helpful to the 'non-traditional' (over twenty-five years old) student as it is to the high school senior. Most scholarship information provided is 'portable,' which means it can be used at any college or university, private or public, within the United States," the company literature explains.

The search results arrive at the student's home within fourteen days if the student is a resident of the continental United States, twenty-one days if a resident of Alaska, Hawaii, Puerto Rico, or Canada. The search firm's results will contain "all known information about the scholarships offered by each source that matches your information, including deadline dates, award amounts, how to request an application, and any other information needed to apply. If the source has information and/or applications available at its web site, information will be listed." FreSch! also includes a copy of their "Scholarship Advice" newsletter that offers guidance with requesting applications, applying for scholarships, and finding other scholarship sources.

The application for a search can be found at the company's web site or by submitting the following application form, "Scholarship Search," with $5.00 to the address shown.

SCHOLARSHIP SEARCH

Mail the completed form with a check or money order in the amount of $5.00 to:
> FreSch! Information Services, LLC,
> Scholarship Search Request,
> 779 Denver Ave., Calhan, CO 80808

Please print your name and address in the following box. This will be used as the shipping label to send you your scholarship search results.

PLEASE PRINT CLEARLY.

Name Mr./Mrs./Ms. _____

Street: _____

City: _____ State: _____ Zip: _____

Telephone Number: _____ Age: _____

Residency:
City: _____ County: _____
State: _____

Marital Status:
- ☐ Single
- ☐ Married
- ☐ Widowed
- ☐ Divorced
- ☐ Separated

Citizenship:
- ☐ U.S. Citizen
- ☐ U.S. Legal Resident Alien ("Green Card")
- ☐ Citizen of another country, in the U.S. on a Student Visa

High School Information:

Name of high school attending, or graduated from: _____

City and State: _____

Year graduated or planning to graduate: _____

Class rank: _____

Check here ☐ if you are a National Merit Scholar Finalist.

Current cumulative GPA *(out of 4.0):* _____

College Plans and Current College Information: _____

Year of study you are seeking scholarship information for:

    ☐ College Freshman

    ☐ College Sophomore

    ☐ College Junior

    ☐ College Senior

    ☐ College Graduate Student, Masters, Doctoral, Post-Doctoral, etc.

    ☐ Full-time student

    ☐ Part-time student

Student Status:

☐ Dependent   ☐ Independent

College presently attending: _____

City and State: _____

If you are a presently a college student, what is your current GPA? _____

If you have already graduated from college, what degree did you receive?

_____

What college do you plan to attend in the future? _____

City and State: _____

Majors/Area of Study:

Type of degree sought:

    ☐ Certificate/Diploma

    ☐ Associate's Degree

    ☐ Bachelor's Degree

    ☐ Master's Degree

    ☐ Doctoral Degree

☐ Post-Doctoral Studies
☐ Other Degree

Proposed major(s):

_____

_____

What is your career goal? _____

_____

Standardized Tests Results:

SAT Scores *(Cumulative, only high school seniors):* _____

SAT II Scores *(Cumulative, only high school seniors):* _____

ACT Scores *(Cumulative, only high school seniors):* _____

GRE Score *(Cumulative, college seniors planning on graduate school):* _____

LSAT Score *(Pre-law students):* _____

MCAT Score *(Pre-med students):* _____

TOEFL Score *(International Students):* _____

Race: _____

Cultural Heritage: (e.g.: Armenian, Greek, German) _____

Disabilities _____

_____

Religious Affiliation: _____

Employment Information:
Note: Many employers offer scholarships to the children of their employees and sometimes

also to their employees. Many companies also offer "tuition reimbursement" programs to their employees to assist with their education. It is strongly recommended that you ask your employer (or have your parents ask their employer) about any scholarships, tuition reimbursement programs, or other financial aid they may offer to employees and their children.

Parent's (s') Occupation: _____
My Occupation: _____

Labor Unions:

If you are a dependent student (under the age of 24) and either of your parents are currently a member of a labor union, or you are (regardless of your age) a member of a labor union, special financial aid may be available. Many labor unions offer scholarships or other financial aid to the children of their members, and sometimes also to their members. In many cases, unions only offer scholarships at the local chapter level. It is strongly recommended that you ask the local chapter of your union (or have your parents ask) about any scholarship or other programs they offer. List below the name of the union you or your parent(s) belongs to.

Parent's (s') Labor Union Membership: _____
My Labor Union Membership: _____

Sorority/Fraternity Membership:

Many sororities and fraternities offer scholarships or other financial aid to their current members. Occasionally, they offer scholarships to dependent children of their members. In many cases, they only offer scholarships at the local chapter level. It is strongly recommended that you ask the local chapter of your sorority or fraternity about any scholarship or other programs they offer.

Parent's (s') Fraternity/Sorority Membership:

_____

My Fraternity/Sorority Membership: _____

Social and Professional Organization Affiliation:

Many social and professional organizations offer scholarships or other financial aid to their members or the dependent children of their current members. Generally, you must have been a member for at least a year, although some organizations will allow you to join at the same time you apply for their scholarship(s). In many cases, the organization will only offer scholarships at the local chapter level. However, it is strongly recommended that you ask about scholarships at every organization you belong to.

Parent's (s') Social and Professional Affiliation:

(e.g., Kiwanis, Lions Club, Boy Scouts of America) _____

My Social and Professional Affiliation: _____

Military Service/Veterans:

Parent is/was member of:	I am/was a member of:	
☐	☐	U.S. Air Force
☐	☐	Air Force ROTC
☐	☐	U.S. Army
☐	☐	Army ROTC
☐	☐	U.S. Navy
☐	☐	U.S. Marine Corps
☐	☐	Coast Guard
☐	☐	Civil Air Patrol
☐	☐	National Guard
☐	☐	POW/MIA, any branch
☐	☐	Killed In Action

Hobbies: _____

_____

Miscellaneous Criteria:

☐ Greater than 6' tall
☐ Left–Handed
☐ Less than 5' tall
☐ Orphan
☐ Single Parent

Other Hobbies/Miscellaneous Criteria:

If you believe there is additional or unique information about yourself, your studies, or your family that will assist us in your scholarship search, please note that below:

_____

_____

Intercollegiate Athletics, Varsity Sports?

List any varsity sports you have played in high school, or intercollegiate sports you have played or are playing in college.

_____

_____

_____

_____

appendix eight

TAX PROVISIONS

Several provisions of the Internal Revenue Service code tax allow students or their parents to receive federal tax benefits in saving for and funding a college education. Taxpayers can receive such benefits as tax deductions, credits, or delayed taxation for funds given to pay for college expenses. Here are several funding programs and their tax implications.

The Hope Scholarship is a federal program that allows a tax credit of $1,500 per year for two years. Taxpayers are eligible for a tax credit equal to 100 percent of the first $1,000 of tuition and 50 percent of the second $1,000 of tuition for the first two years of college, less any grant aid. The credit may be claimed in two taxable years but not beyond the year the student completes his or her first two years of college.

The program has three major disadvantages:

1. The tax credit begins to be phased out when family income reaches an adjusted gross income $80,000 for joint filers, and beginning at $40,000 for those who file individually.

2. Students or parents who have saved for tuition with EE Savings Bonds will no longer be eligible for tax-free interest when using the Hope Scholarship.

3. The Hope may not be used with the new education IRA.

The Lifetime Learning Credit is basically an extension of the Hope Scholarship for juniors, seniors, graduate students, and those taking classes full-time or part-time to improve or upgrade their job skills, such as vocational tech school training and advanced graduate studies. The program provides a 20 percent tax credit for the $5,000 of tuition and fees paid each year through 2002. Assuming the federal government continues to fund the program, the tax credit after 2002 becomes 20 percent of the first $10,000 in tuition and fees. The Lifetime Learning Credit program phases out at the same income levels as the Hope Scholarship.

The Education IRA allows families with children under age eighteen to deposit up to $500 per child, per year into an educational IRA. Earnings are tax-free as are withdrawals when used for postsecondary expenses, including tuition, fees, books, equipment, room, and board. Begun early in the child's life, the tax-free earnings benefit from compounding, growing to triple their investment after eighteen years, based on a 10 percent return.

The program has three major disadvantages:

1. The program begins to be phased out for families with combined adjusted gross incomes of $150,000 for joint filers and $95,000 for those who file individually.

2. The Education IRA may not be used in the same year with the Hope Scholarship or Lifetime Learning Credit.

3. If the money in the special IRA is not used for higher education expenses, the withdrawals are subject to income taxes and a 10 percent penalty. Parents may wish to investigate the benefits provided by a Uniform Gift to Minors Account (UGMA) noted in chapter 10.

The Roth IRA, although not primarily a college savings account, can work effectively to save money that way. Individuals can put in as much as $2,000 per year as noted; $4,000 for couples whose income is $150,000 or less. (Singles income max is $95,000.) The higher deposit level compared with the $500 maximum of the Education IRA will mean more funds accumulating tax-free for a college education. In addition, all or some of the funds from the Roth IRA can be left for retirement or other needs, although a penalty will occur if withdrawn early. However, there is no penalty for early withdrawal when used for educational expenses.

The key disadvantage is that the deposits are taxable; parents have to pay the taxes ahead of time when they are in a higher tax bracket. The advantage is that the investor doesn't have to pay taxes on the growth.

The Student Loan Interest Deduction allows parents of dependent students as well as students classified as independent to deduct the interest paid on their student loans from their federal income taxes. This includes loans (both private and government-backed) for tuition, fees, books, equipment, room, and board. The maximum deductible interest for the year 2000 is $2,000 and for each year after that, $2,500.

This program has two major disadvantages:

1. The deduction is good on new and existing loans but only for the first sixty months of repayment.
2. The tax benefit begins to be phased out for families with an adjusted gross income of $60,000 for joint filers and $40,000 for single filers.

The Traditional IRA. Taxpayers may now withdraw funds from a standard investment retirement account without penalty when used for postsecondary education expenses for spouse, child, grandchild, and/or the taxpayer. The maximum withdrawal cannot exceed the total cost of education including tuition, fees, room and board, etc.

Employer-Paid Benefits allow an employee to deduct up to $5,200 on employer-provided education expenses, under section 127 of the current Internal Revenue Service tax code. (For more information, review page 81.)

Expanded benefits for prepaid tuition plans now allow interest on earnings to be taxed only at the time of withdrawal for all state-sponsored prepaid tuition plans. Students using the plans are also eligible for the Hope Scholarship or Lifetime Learning tax credits.

appendix nine

APPLYING FOR THE ROBERT C. BYRD SCHOLARSHIP

Most states have a special office administering the Robert C. Byrd Honors Scholarship. (Check the phone directory for any address, area code, or phone number changes.)

ALABAMA
Department of Education
50 North Ripley Street
Montgomery, AL 36130
(334) 242-9950

ALASKA
Department of Education
801 West 10th Street
Juneau, AK 99801
(907) 465-8715

ARIZONA
Department of Education
1535 West Jefferson
Phoenix, AZ 85007
(602) 542-3053

ARKANSAS
Department of Education
4 State Capitol Mall
Little Rock, AR 72201
(501) 682-4474

CALIFORNIA
Student Aid Commission
1515 S Street, North Building
Sacramento, CA 94245
(916) 322-2294

COLORADO
Department of Education
201 East Colfax Avenue
Denver, CO 80203
(303) 866-6779

CONNECTICUT
Department of Higher Education
61 Woodland Street
Hartford, CT 06105
(860) 566-3910

DELAWARE
State Department of Instruction
P.O. Box 1402
Dover, DE 19903
(302) 739-5622

DISTRICT OF COLUMBIA
District of Columbia Schools
4501 Lee Street, NE
Washington, DC 20019
(202) 724-4934

FLORIDA
Florida Department of Education
255 Collins
Tallahassee, FL 32399
(904) 488-1034

GEORGIA
State Department of Education
205 Butler Street
Atlanta, GA 30334
(404) 656-5812

HAWAII
Hawaii Department of Education
2530 10th Avenue
Honolulu, HI 96816
(808) 733-9103

IDAHO
State Board of Education
650 West State Street
Boise, ID 83720
(208) 334-2113

ILLINOIS
Assistance Commission
1755 Lake Cook Road
Deerfield, IL 60015
(847) 948-8500

INDIANA
Department of Education
State House, Room 229
Indianapolis, IN 46204
(317) 232-2350

IOWA
Student Aid Commission
914 Grand Ave., Suite 201
Des Moines, IA 50309
(800) 383-4222

KANSAS
Department of Education
120 East Tenth Street
Topeka, KS 66612
(913) 296-4876

KENTUCKY
Department of Education
1919 Capital Plaza Tower
Frankfort, KY 40601
(502) 564-3421

LOUISIANA
Department of Education
P.O. Box 94064
Baton Rouge, LA 70804
(504) 342-2098

MAINE
Finance Authority of Maine
P.O. Box 949
Augusta, ME 04332
(207) 287-2183

MARYLAND
State Department of Education
200 West Baltimore Street
Baltimore, MD 21201
(410) 767-0480

MASSACHUSETTS
State Department of Education
350 Main Street
Malden, MA 02148
(617) 388-3300

MICHIGAN
Higher Education Authority
P.O. Box 30462
Lansing, MI 48909
(517) 373-3394

MINNESOTA
State Department of Education
712 Capitol Square Building
St. Paul, MN 55101
(612) 282-5088

MISSISSIPPI
State Department of Education
P.O. Box 771
Jackson, MS 39205
(601) 359-3768

MISSOURI
Secondary Education Department.
P.O. Box 480
Jefferson City, MO 65102
(314) 751-2931

MONTANA
Office of Public Instruction
State Capitol, Room 106
Helena, MT 59620
(406) 444-4422

NEBRASKA
Department of Education
P.O. Box 94987
Lincoln, NE 68509
(402) 471-2784

NEVADA
Department of Education
400 West King Street
Carson City, NV 89710
(702) 687-3100

NEW HAMPSHIRE
Department of Education
101 Pleasant Street
Concord, NH 03301
(603) 271-2632

NEW JERSEY
Department of Education
225 West State Street
Trenton, NJ 08625
(609) 984-6409

NEW MEXICO
Department of Education
300 Don Gaspar
Santa Fe, NM 87501
(505) 827-6648

NEW YORK
State Education Department
111 Educational Building
Albany, NY 12234
(518) 474-5705

NORTH CAROLINA
State Department of Instruction
116 West Edenton Street
Raleigh, NC 27603
(919) 715-1161

NORTH DAKOTA
Department of Public Instruction
State Capitol Building
Bismarck, ND 58505
(701) 224-2271

OHIO
State Department of Education
65 So. Front Street, Room 1005
Columbus, OH 43266
(614) 466-2761

OKLAHOMA
State Department of Education
2500 North Lincoln Boulevard
Oklahoma City, OK 73105
(405) 521-4122

OREGON
Department of Education
700 Pringle Parkway, SE
Salem, OR 97310
(503) 378-5585

PENNSYLVANIA
Higher Education Agency
P.O. Box 8114
Harrisburg, PA 17105
(717) 783-2862

RHODE ISLAND
State Department of Education
22 Hayes Street
Providence, RI 02908
(401) 277-3126

SOUTH CAROLINA
Department of Education
1429 Senate Street
Columbia, SC 29201
(803) 734-8364

SOUTH DAKOTA
Department of Education
700 Governors Drive
Pierre, SD 57501
(605) 773-3134

TENNESSEE
Department of Education
100 Cordell Hull Building
Nashville, TN 37219
(615) 741-1346

TEXAS
Texas Education Agency
1701 North Congress
Austin, TX 78701
(512) 483-6340

UTAH
State Office of Education
250 East 500 South
Salt Lake City, UT 84111
(801) 538-7779

VERMONT
Student Assistance
P.O. Box 2000
Winooski, VT 05404
(800) 642-3177

VIRGINIA
Department of Education
P.O. Box 2120
Richmond, VA 23216
(804) 225-2072

WASHINGTON
Department of Public Instruction
Old Capitol Building
Olympia, WA 98504
(360) 753-2858

WEST VIRGINIA
Education Grant Program
P.O. Box 4007
Charleston, WV 25364
(304) 347-1266

WISCONSIN
Department of Public Instruction
P.O. Box 7841
Madison, WI 53707
(608) 266-2364

WYOMING
Department of Education
2300 Capitol Avenue
Cheyenne, WY 82002
(307) 777-6265

GUAM
University of Guam
303 University Drive
Mangiloa, Guam 96923
(671) 472-8524

PUERTO RICO
Department of Education
P.O. Box 759
Hato Rey, Puerto Rico 00919
(809) 753-1623

VIRGIN ISLANDS
Department of Education
No. 44-46 Kongens Gade,
Charlotte Amalie
St. Thomas, Virgin Islands 00802
(809) 774-0100

ESSAY PREPARATION

The following article on essay preparation offers key insights for students. "Writing an Essay," by John C. Conkright, dean of admissions at Randolph-Macon College (Ashland, Virginia), is a brochure published by the college. It is reprinted below with permission of the author.

If you are like most students, you see the college essay as just another hurdle you must jump on the way to being accepted at the college of your choice. In fact, the essay is a rare *opportunity* to "talk" directly to the college's admissions committee and help them see you as a thinking and feeling person, rather than simply a set of impersonal statistics. Except for the interview, it is your only chance to share your thoughts, insights, and opinions, and highlight your maturity and outlook on life. If you see the college essay as an opportunity—then it is clearly worth the extra effort and time put forth in writing it.

The college essay is extremely important for two major reasons: First of all, it enables the college admissions office to personally evaluate your communications skills and your ability to convey your thoughts. Secondly, it enables them to learn more about you as a person. A well-written essay can speak worlds about your attitudes, feelings, personal qualities, imagination and creativity.

Many schools will either give you a topic to write about or present several specific topics from which you must choose. Others may simply suggest general topics or give you total freedom to write about something that interests or concerns you.

Here are a few hints about approaching your topic:

- Narrow your topic and try to be as specific and illustrative as possible.
- The easiest topic to write about is you. If you choose to write about yourself, remember that little incidents and facts are often the most revealing concerning character and outlook.
- Do not be afraid to write about something that you think is a little different. A unique topic or approach is often refreshing to a college admissions officer.

Before sitting down to write your essay, spend some time organizing your thoughts. Develop a framework for your essay so it will have a logical progression from one idea to the next. Consider your purpose in writing, what you want to convey, and the tone that you think is most appropriate for the topic. Decide on a style that is comfortable for you, not one that you think the college admissions committee prefers.

Remember, you do not have to get it right the first time! Instead, write the first draft with the main focus on content. Then set it aside for a day or two, reread it with a fresh perspective, and make any necessary changes including organization, style, grammar and spelling.

Once you have rewritten your first draft, you may wish to try it out on your family, friends and English teacher or guidance counselor. While the final product and final "voice" should be yours, they may be able to offer helpful suggestions for improvement.

Here are some "dos" and "don'ts" that may help you:

- Do think "small" and write about something you know well.
- Do show rather than tell.
- Do write in your own "voice" and style.
- Don't write what you think others want to read.
- Don't exaggerate or write to impress.
- Don't use a flowery, inflated or pretentious style.
- Don't neglect the technical part of your essay (grammar, spelling and sentence structure).
- Don't ramble—say what you have to say and conclude.

Your college essay, along with your high school record, standardized test scores and extracurricular involvement, will provide the basis upon which the college makes its admissions decision.

A well-written essay can affect that final decision in a very positive way. Keep this in mind and take full advantage of the *opportunity* which the college essay affords you.

SAMPLE STUDENT LOAN PAYMENTS

FEDERAL PERKINS LOAN

(No Loan Origination Fee)

Plan	Loan	Interest Rate	Monthly	Total*	Cumulative Percent
10 years	$ 5,000	5%	$ 53	$ 6,364	27.3%
10 years	10,000	5	106	12,728	27.3
10 years	15,000	5	159	19,092	27.3
10 years	20,000	5	212	25,457	27.3
10 years	40,000	5	424	50,914	27.3

*Represents loan plus total interest and origination fees paid over life of the loan.

FEDERAL STAFFORD LOANS

(Totals Include 4% Loan Origination Fee Previously Paid)

Plan	Loan	Interest Rate	Monthly	Total*	Cumulative Percent
10 years	$ 5,000	8.25%	$ 61	$ 7,560	51.2%
10 years	10,000	8.25	123	15,118	51.2
10 years	15,000	8.25	184	22,678	51.2
10 years	20,000	8.25	245	30,237	51.2
15 years	$ 5,000	8.25%	$ 49	$ 8,932	78.6%
15 years	10,000	8.25	97	17,863	78.6
15 years	15,000	8.25	146	26,794	78.6
15 years	20,000	8.25	194	35,725	78.6
20 years	$ 5,000	8.25%	$ 43	$10,424	108.5%
20 years	10,000	8.25	85	20,850	108.5
20 years	15,000	8.25	128	31,274	108.5
20 years	20,000	8.25	170	41,698	108.5
20 years	30,000	8.25	255	62,548	108.5
20 years	40,000	8.25	340	83,396	108.5
20 years	50,000	8.25	426	104,252	108.5

*Represents loan amount plus total interest and origination fees paid over life of the loan.

A SAMPLE BUDGET

As noted in chapter 9, every student needs to set up a budget both to have a spending plan, and to graduate with little debt. Below is a sample budget for a student with $1,735 every month. This sample monthly budget is followed by a blank budget worksheet you may copy and use for your own spending plan.

SUGGESTED SPENDING PLAN CATEGORIES

($15,615 per year estimate includes tuition, room and board, travel, etc.)

TOTAL AVAILABLE FUNDS:		$ 1735
Salary or tips if employed	280	
Savings or Checking	100	
Parents	380	
Loans & Scholarships	975	
Other		
LESS TITHE & APPLICABLE TAXES:	$ 173	
EQUALS NET AVAILABLE FUNDS:	$ 1562	
LESS MONTHLY EXPENSES:		
Housing Costs		$ 274
Rent/Mortgage	211	

Utilities	26
Telephone	37

(Divide totals by number of roommates)

Food Allowance	$ 265
Tuition & Fees	$ 440
Books	$ 35

(Divide annual totals by nine months)

Transportation Expenses $ 201

Car Payments	122
Car Insurance	Dad
Gas & Oil	44
Car Repairs	35

Clothing Allowance $ 40

Entertainment $ 80

Restaurants	30
Movie Rentals	12
Social Events	38

Medical Allowance $ 10

Doctor	Ins
Dentist	Dad
Prescriptions	10
Other	

Debts $ 20

Credit Cards	
Loans	
Revolving	20
Other	

Insurance (other than car) $

Savings (Bank/Mutual Funds, etc.) $ 20

Miscellaneous $ 177

Gifts	12
Cosmetics/Shaving	26
Haircuts	28
Laundry	18

Cleaning Supplies	_18_
Fraternity/Sorority Dues	_30_
Music Supplies	_10_
Art Supplies	_____
Extra Date Money	_25_
Other	_10_

Child Care (If Applicable) $ _____

School Tuition	_____
Transportation	_____
Day Care	_____
Baby-sitting	_____
Diapers/Supplies	_____

TOTAL EXPENSES $ 1735

DIFFERENCE PER MONTH $ 0

BUDGET WORKSHEETS

SUGGESTED SPENDING PLAN CATEGORIES

TOTAL AVAILABLE FUNDS: $ _____
Salary or tips if employed   _____
    Savings or Checking   _____
    Parents   _____
    Loans & Scholarships   _____
    Other   _____

LESS TITHE & APPLICABLE TAXES: $ _____
EQUALS NET AVAILABLE FUNDS: $ _____

    LESS MONTHLY EXPENSES:

Housing Costs $ _____
    Rent/Mortgage   _____
    Utilities   _____
    Telephone   _____
    (Divide totals by number of roommates)

Food Allowance $ _____
Tuition & Fees $ _____
Books $ _____
    (Divide annual totals by nine months)

Transportation Expenses $ _____
    Car Payments   _____
    Car Insurance   _____
    Gas & Oil   _____
    Car Repairs   _____

Clothing Allowance $ _____

Entertainment $ _____
    Restaurants   _____
    Movie Rentals   _____
    Social Events   _____

Medical Allowance $ _____
    Doctor   _____
    Dentist   _____

Prescriptions   _____

Other   _____

Debts $ _____

     Credit Cards   _____

     Loans   _____

     Revolving   _____

     Other   _____

Insurance (other than car) $ _____

Savings (Bank/Mutual Funds, etc.) $ _____

Miscellaneous $ _____

     Gifts   _____

     Cosmetics/Shaving   _____

     Haircuts   _____

     Laundry   _____

     Cleaning Supplies   _____

     Fraternity/Sorority Dues   _____

     Music Supplies   _____

     Art Supplies   _____

     Extra Date Money   _____

     Other   _____

Child Care (If Applicable) $ _____

     School Tuition   _____

     Transportation   _____

     Day Care   _____

     Baby-sitting   _____

     Diapers/Supplies   _____

TOTAL EXPENSES $ _____

DIFFERENCE PER MONTH $ _____

PROJECTED COSTS AND NECESSARY SAVINGS FOR COLLEGE

The cost of a college education is projected to continue its steady march upward during the next two decades. Parents who develop a pattern of steadily saving for a child will reap dividends years later. The following charts show the upward trend in college costs through the year 2015, as well as give parents guidelines for saving to meet those projected costs. For all four charts that follow, these are assumptions and not a guarantee of future performance. Illustration is for planning assistance only and is not intended to project the performance of any specific investment vehicle.

The illustration below shows near-term cost projections at a public college. If parents have a child age twelve in the year 2000, they would be able to pay the projected cost of $75,600 for four years of education by making consecutive monthly investments of $473 until the child reaches eighteen. This assumes annual compounding at 12 percent and no withdrawals.

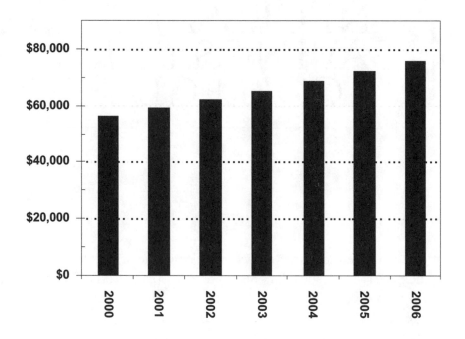

**PROJECTED COSTS FOR FOUR YEARS
AT A PUBLIC COLLEGE,
ENTERING 2000 THROUGH 2006**

Source: Adapted from "Planning for College," a brochure from Met Life Resources of Metropolitan Life Insurance Co., 1996. Annual increases have been adjusted based on a 5 percent rate of inflation.

The illustration below shows near-term cost projections at a private college. If parents have a child age twelve in the year 2000, they would be able to pay the projected cost of $148,900 for four years of education by making consecutive monthly investments of $931 until the child reaches eighteen. This assumes annual compounding at 12 percent and no withdrawals.

**PROJECTED COSTS FOR FOUR YEARS
AT A PRIVATE COLLEGE,
ENTERING 2000 THROUGH 2006**

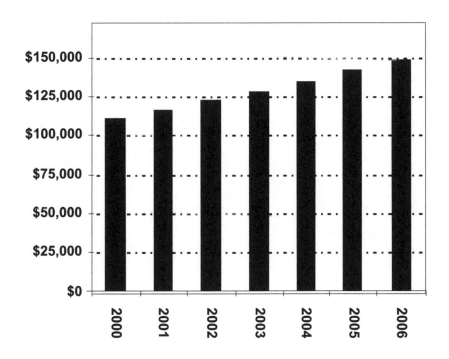

Source: Adapted from "Planning for College," a brochure from Met Life Resources of Metropolitan Life Insurance Co., 1996. Annual increases have been adjusted based on a 5 percent rate of inflation.

The illustration below shows near-term cost projections at a public college. If parents have a child age three in the year 2000, they would be able to pay the projected cost of $117,400 for four years of education by making consecutive monthly investments of $177 until the child reaches eighteen. This assumes annual compounding at 12 percent and no withdrawals.

**PROJECTED COSTS FOR FOUR YEARS
AT A PUBLIC COLLEGE,
ENTERING 2000 THROUGH 2015**

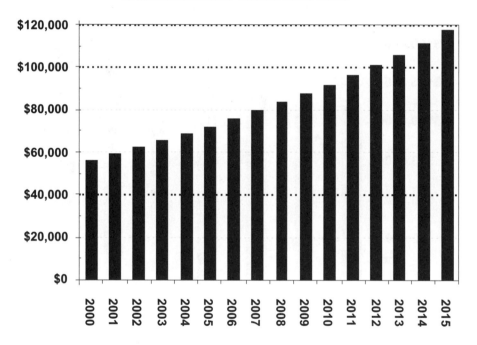

Source: Adapted from "Planning for College," a brochure from Met Life Resources of Metropolitan Life Insurance Co., 1996. Annual increases have been adjusted based on a 5 percent rate of inflation.

The illustration below shows long-term cost projections at a private college. If parents have a child age three in the year 2000, they would be able to pay the projected cost of $231,000 for four years of education by making consecutive monthly investments of $359 until the child reaches eighteen. This assumes annual compounding at 12 percent and no withdrawals.

PROJECTED COSTS FOR FOUR YEARS AT A PRIVATE COLLEGE, ENTERING 2000 THROUGH 2015

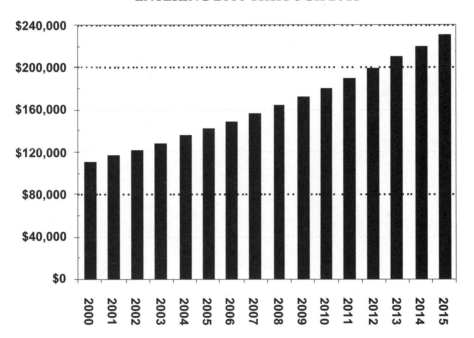

Source: Adapted from "Planning for College," a brochure from Met Life Resources of Metropolitan Life Insurance Co., 1996. Annual increases have been adjusted based on a 5 percent rate of inflation.

appendix fourteen

PREPAID TUITION PROGRAMS

The following states have a prepaid tuition plan or college savings plan in effect:

PREPAID PLANS

Alabama 800-252-7228

Colorado 800-478-5651

Illinois 877-877-3724

Maryland 888-463-4723

Michigan 800-638-4543

Nevada 888-477-2667

Ohio 800-233-6734

Pennsylvania 800-440-4000

Tennessee 888-486-2378

Virginia 888-567-0540

West Virginia 800-307-4701

Alaska 800-478-0003

Florida 800-552-4723

Maine 877-668-1116

Massachusetts 800-449-6332

Mississippi 800-987-4450

New Mexico 800-279-9777

Oregon 503-378-4329

South Carolina 888-772-4723

Texas 800-445-4723

Washington 877-438-8848

STATE SAVINGS PLANS

Arizona 602-229-2592

California 877-728-4338

Colorado 800-478-5651

Connecticut 888-799-2438

Delaware 800-292-7935

Florida 800-552-4723

Hawaii 808-586-1518

Illinois 217-782-1319

Indiana 888-814-6800

Iowa 888-446-6696

Kansas 785-296-3171

Kentucky 800-336-0318

Louisiana 800-259-5626

Maine 877-668-1116

Massachusetts 800-544-2776

Minnesota 800-657-3806

Missouri 888-414-6678

Montana 800-888-2723

New Hampshire 800-544-1722

New Jersey 877-465-2378

New York 877-697-2837

North Carolina 800-600-3453

Oklahoma 405-858-4422

Rhode Island 877-474-4378

Tennessee 888-486-2378

Utah 800-418-2551

Vermont 800-642-3177

Virginia 888-567-0540

Wisconsin 888-338-3789

Wyoming 307-777-7408

Moody Press, a ministry of the Moody Bible Institute,
is designed for education, evangelization, and edification.
If we may assist you in knowing more about Christ
and the Christian life, please write us without obligation:
Moody Press, c/o MLM, Chicago, Illinois 60610.